KU-350-802

BEYOND THE ZULU PRINCIPLE

WARNING

Stockmarket investments, and the income from them, can go down as well as up. They may also have poor marketability. When you seek advice, also ask about marketability. The shares referred to in the text of this book are for illustrative purposes only and are not an invitation to deal in them. The book was completed in August 1996 and since then market conditions have changed. Neither the publishers nor the author accept any legal responsibility for the contents of the work, which is not a substitute for detailed professional advice. Readers should conduct their investment activity through an appropriately authorized person.

BEYOND THE ZULU PRINCIPLE

EXTRAORDINARY PROFITS FROM GROWTH SHARES

JIM SLATER

CARTOONS BY

ORION BUSINESS
BOOKS

To Helen, who has always been a long-term Hold

Copyright © 1996, 1998 Jim Slater
Cartoons Copyright © 1994, 1996

All rights reserved

The right of Jim Slater to be identified as the
author of this work has been asserted by him in accordance with
the Copyright, Designs and Patents Act 1988.

Hardback edition first published in Great Britain in 1996
This paperback edition first published in Great Britain in 1998
by Orion Business
An imprint of The Orion Publishing Group Ltd
Orion House, 5 Upper St Martin's Lane, London WC2H 9EA

A CIP catalogue record for this book
is available from the British Library.

ISBN 0–75281–385–4

Printed in Great Britain by
Butler & Tanner Ltd, Frome and London

CONTENTS

ACKNOWLEDGEMENTS

I would like to thank Peter Scott, Graham Quick and Chris Cole of Hemmington Scott for their help in editing this book and contributing to it. Many of the lessons learned when working together on *Company REFS* as a team effort are incorporated in the text. I would also like to thank my son, Mark, for editing this book and making many helpful suggestions.

Particular thanks are due to Tom Stevenson, City Editor of the *Independent*, for editing the final version and making many constructive suggestions for improving both the text and structure of most of the chapters.

As always, I must congratulate Edward McLachlan, who has drawn the superb cartoons. For reasons that will become apparent, my favourite is on page 191.

I would also like to thank my wife for understanding that writing takes up a lot of time that might otherwise be spent with her.

I would feel unsafe if I did not thank my secretary, Pam Hall, who is now a veteran of all of my investment books. Most of the chapters have to be typed many times before we reach a final draft. As always, Pam has been a tower of strength.

Last, but not least, thanks are due to Lesley Baxter for line-editing the final version with me. She always makes an invaluable contribution.

PREFACE TO THE PAPERBACK EDITION

Since writing the hardback version of *Beyond The Zulu Principle* there have been a number of important developments.

First and foremost, I am now in possession of powerful additional evidence showing the effectiveness of the investment criteria outlined in this book. The details are set out in the Appendix on page 208. I think you will find them very convincing.

Since the publication of the hardback in 1996, I have held two investment classes for beginners; one on 28 September and the other on 16 November 1997. I am unlikely to hold any more, although I will probably continue to speak at seminars like Sharelink's and those organised by the *Financial Mail on Sunday*.

I will in future be concentrating on Intermediate and Masterclasses. If you are interested in attending one of these, please contact 0171 835 0240 for further details.

The new electonic version of *Company REFS* (CD REFS) is now available on CD-ROM. This enables subscribers with a computer to obtain all the details of REFS in the Companies Volume and make their own tailor-made searches for interesting shares. Special terms are available for subscribers who want to take both the written and electronic version. For further details contact Hemmington Scott on 0171 278 7769.

I am thinking of writing a regular monthly newsletter. If I do, it would incorporate the following features:

1. Comment on the market as a whole.

2. A strongly argued recommendation (when opportunities could be identified) in each of the three main categories: one from the top 350 companies, one from the SmallCap index and one from the Fledgling index or from AIM.

3. A carefully tailored search each month of the vast Hemmington Scott database. The introduction of CD REFS gives me great flexibility to make demanding searches using my own highly selective criteria. Each month, I would conduct a search of this nature, explain the criteria I adopted, and review the findings in detail.

4. Points of interest. These would include book reviews, guest contributions from investors of note and thought-provoking items I have noticed in the world press.

5. Monthly updates. Once companies had been recommended, their progress and newsflow would be carefully monitored and reported on so investors became quickly aware of any changes in the 'story'.

6. Monthly reviews of companies affected by key active investment measures. These would include relative strength, changes in brokers' consensus forecasts or directors' dealings.

7. Readers' questions together with my answers. I would only feature letters when they asked questions that would be of real interest to all readers.

If you are interested and want to know if I have proceeded with the idea of a newsletter, I suggest that you contact Hemmington Scott.

I have recently started an Internet site which explains my investment approach, offers current recommended reading, gives details of REFS and my masterclasses and provides the answers to most frequently asked questions. If you are interested I suggest that you pay the site a visit. The website address is http://www.global-investor.com/slater and the service is of course, free.

I hope you enjoy this book and that it will help to refine and improve your investment approach. Perhaps the best advice I can give you is to bear in mind the wise words of the American Will Rogers – 'Buy some good stock. Hold it 'til it goes up ... and then sell it. If it doesn't go up, don't buy it!'

Jim Slater, *December, 1997*

1
—
YOUR APPROACH TO INVESTMENT

Good investment is often a case of turning conventional wisdom on its head, so let me say at the outset who this book is *not* for. If you have a pension and some life insurance, and maybe a unit trust or two, and if you are happy with the steady, relatively secure growth they provide, this book will probably not interest you.

You will be reassured by the low risk of your pooled investments, and the fact that their performance is broadly in line with the stock market as a whole. You probably don't want to spend too much time worrying about your finances.

Now, don't misunderstand me, there is nothing wrong with that approach – everyone needs to provide a secure financial foundation for themselves and their dependants, and not everyone is prepared to devote a significant proportion of their free time to investment.

If, however, you want more than the average returns offered by passive investments such as unit and investment trusts; *if* you are prepared to set aside a few hours a week to achieve those *extra*-ordinary returns; and *if* you believe, as I do, that you will enjoy doing so, then this book is for you.

I have devoted a substantial amount of my time in recent years to fine-tuning my thoughts on investment and I am very excited about the conclusions I have now reached. I have also enjoyed very good financial returns putting my investment theories into practice; I hope that after reading this book you will too.

You won't find a get-rich-quick formula in these pages. But I really believe that you *will* find a tested approach to investment that will give you a good chance of beating professional investors and the market by a substantial margin, year in, year out. You will also derive a great deal of enjoyment and satisfaction along the way.

AIM TO BEAT THE INSTITUTIONS

Most people's first thought is that it would be difficult, if not impossible, to match the performance of professional fund managers. They devote their working lives to investment; they ought to be experts. Bear in mind, however, that investment managers are different from the qualified practitioners at the top of many other professions. Unlike doctors, barristers, architects and accountants, they do not have to study for five or more years, read hundreds of books on their subject and pass a series of difficult examinations. In investment management, it is possible to get by with very little theoretical knowledge and no formal qualifications of any kind. The competition is therefore not so daunting to the private investor as might appear at first sight.

All investors start at a disadvantage when trying to outperform the market. Unlike the indices, all investors have to pay dealing costs and investors in institutional funds have to pay initial and annual management charges. You may be surprised to learn that, for the institutions, these difficulties contribute to lamentable performance figures – less than 10% of fund managers are capable of beating the market on a regular basis. Even when the playing field is level, the institutions are weak opponents and, as it happens, there are several areas where the small private investor actually has an advantage.

Warren Buffett, probably the world's most successful investor, sums up one of the institutions' problems well: 'A fat wallet is the enemy of superior investment results. Though there are as many good businesses as ever, it is useless for us to make purchases that are inconsequential in relation to [our] capital. We now consider a security for purchase only if we believe we can deploy at least $100m in it. Given that minimum [our] investment universe has shrunk dramatically.' In other words, there are some companies that are too small for the institutions to bother about investing in even if they believe that the shares will outperform the market by a wide margin.

The private investors' 'universe' is much wider than that of any institution. This is a considerable advantage – with less money to deploy, they can invest *meaningfully* in smaller companies. As you will see later, expertise is needed and there are greater risks. However, on average over the last 40 years or so, small companies have performed about 4% per annum better than the market. This may not sound very much, but the average return on equities (with dividends reinvested) has been about 12% per annum over the last 75 years. The compounding of an extra 4% would have added a meaningful amount to overall investment performance. Investments growing at 12% per annum take six years to double – growing at 16%, they take only 4½ years.

So, the first advantage of private investors is one of size. The second is one of spread. Not many institutions have to invest as much as Warren Buffett, but in the UK there are several unit and investment trusts with billions under management. Certainly £100m is not in the least bit exceptional, which results in a typical trust's portfolio having to be spread over as many as 500 shares. Private investors know that, even with a portfolio of ten shares, their first choice is better than their tenth. Obviously, their tenth selection is far better than their hundredth and the five-hundredth does not even bear comparison.

In fact, it is very difficult in the UK to find as many as 100 prime growth shares. Most active private investors need to invest in only about ten at any one time, so they have a very substantial further advantage over institutional investors.

The third important edge of private investors is that their 'circle of competence' can be more meaningfully applied to a small portfolio. Everyone knows something special. It may arise from a hobby or interest, through a job or just from noticing what is happening in their local environment. A computer buff, for example, might be aware of new developments in networking; an insurance broker would understand the problems facing Lloyds and know the companies most likely to be taken over in the industry; and most people would notice if a new kind of restaurant or shop in their locality was becoming increasingly popular, or if a nearby factory was laying off some of its work force or expanding in a big way.

Everyone has a circle of competence, but active private investors can apply it to the relatively small number of shares in their portfolios, so the impact can be substantial. The institutional manager's circle of competence may be greater, but his portfolio contains so many shares that the effect is diluted. The private investor's circle of competence is spread like a pat of butter on just one slice of toast, whereas the fund manager's pat has to be spread over hundreds.

INVESTMENT CLUBS

Investment clubs can be an excellent source of help and inspiration for private investors and sharing the fun with others can increase their enjoyment as well as improving their performance. The legal maximum for members is 20, which might include the manager of a restaurant, a solicitor, an accountant, an estate agent, several married women and perhaps someone in public relations. Every one of these people brings to the group their own circle of competence to add to its overall strength and know-how.

There are other advantages too. Within every club there is always a 'faster gun' – someone who knows more about investment than the other members and can add to the knowledge of the group. Also, in a club it is easier to stick to a discipline and to gain moral support from other members. Last but not least, the cost of newsletters and necessary investment services like *Company REFS* can be shared to reduce the expense to a very affordable level per member.

Anyone interested in joining an investment club, or forming one, should contact ProShare, Library Chambers, 13–14 Basinghall Street, London EC2V 5BQ (Tel: 0171 600 0984). In particular, they should obtain a copy of the ProShare manual, which costs £25 and explains everything they need to know.

THE ZULU PRINCIPLE

Private investors can also develop their investment expertise by applying the Zulu Principle. This was the name of my first book on investment, taken from an idea I had after observing my wife read a four-page article in *Reader's Digest* on the subject of Zulus. As a result, within a few minutes she knew more than I did about Zulus and it occurred to me that, if she had then borrowed all the available books on Zulus from the local library, she would have become the leading expert in Surrey. If she had subsequently been invited to stay on a Zulu kraal (by an unsuspecting chief) and read about the history of Zulus at Johannesburg University for another six months, she would have become one of the leading experts in the world.

The key point is that my wife would have applied a disproportionate effort to becoming relatively expert in a very narrow subject. She would have used a laser beam rather than a scattergun and her intellectual and other resources would, in that narrow context, have been used to maximum advantage. So it is with investment – concentrate on an approach, such as buying growth shares or asset situations, or concentrate on a particular sector. That way, you will become relatively expert in your chosen area. It is only necessary to be six inches taller than the other people in a room to see above everyone's heads. Applying the Zulu Principle helps you grow those extra six inches.

I suggest that for most private investors their first (and possibly final) area of specialisation should be growth shares. They are by far the most rewarding investments. The upside is unlimited and, if the right companies are picked, the shares can be held for many years, during which they should multiply the original stake many times.

Cyclicals are a different ball game. The aim is to buy them at the bottom of the cycle and sell near the top. The main problem is getting the timing right and then deciding when to reinvest.

Growth shares are far more relaxing, so this book will concentrate on them.

READING ABOUT INVESTMENT

There is no doubt that, as a first step, aspiring investors should read as much as possible about investment. In other fields, such as chemistry, medicine, law and accountancy, there are hundreds of British books covering every aspect of these subjects. Investment is different – there are plenty of excellent American books on investment but hardly any British ones. Maybe that is because the art of money-making is more admired in America, where it has become an important part of the national culture. Or perhaps it is because in the UK people feel that the subject of investment is dull and dry. Whatever the reason, in order to dig deeply into investment strategy and tactics, we have to rely upon books imported from America.

Most people who have never cooked before and want to become expert, would at least think about reading a cookery book. Investment is no different. You should read as much as possible about the subject before investing. I have devoted the whole of Chapter 19 to investment reading. Anyone who reads the majority of the books I recommend should quickly gain an important edge over other investors – remember, in the kingdom of the blind the one-eyed man is king.

There are three British primers: *Beginner's Guide to Investment* by Bernard Gray, *How to Read the Financial Pages* by Michael Brett, and my own book *Investment Made Easy*. All of these give a good grounding in investment and are available in paperback. From this point onwards, I shall assume that readers have studied at least one of them and understand the meaning of terms like price-earnings ratio, dividend yield and scrip issue. I shall also work on the assumption that they have read *The Zulu Principle*, or at least one other investment book of a similar standard. This will enable me to write at a brisker pace, avoid treading old ground and save boring more experienced readers to death.

COMPANY REFS

In addition to general strategic and tactical advice on investment, active private investors need a regular monthly or quarterly flow of reliable investment statistics. In conjunction with Hemmington Scott, the City information and research organisation and publisher of *The Hambro Company Guide*, I have devised a new service, *Company REFS* (REFS), to meet this requirement. I make no apology for advertising REFS here. In my view, and that of the many investors who use it to great effect, it is the definitive single-source investment tool. Private investors can now obtain all the financial statistics and other information they need from one source. The companies volume covers every quoted company (excluding investment trusts) with a very comprehensive full-page company entry including a chart and all of the key financial statistics for the last five years. In addition, whenever available, it shows the consensus of brokers' forecasts for the next two years together with the individual brokers' forecasts and details of their buy, sell or hold recommendations.

The tables volume contains directors' dealings during the last six months, brokers' consensus forecast changes during the month, chief executive officer changes and over 80 pages of tables seeking to identify investment anomalies. For example, there are tables of shares with attractive price-earnings ratios, price-earnings growth factors, net asset values, cash flows, dividend yields etc., and detailed sector statistics highlighting the exact position of each company in its peer group and in the market as a whole.

I learned a great deal from the research necessary to devise REFS and from the experience of developing the service. As a result, many of my original criteria have been modified. As we go along, I will not always draw attention to the changes in my thinking; in most cases I will simply outline my ideas as they are today.

In the following chapters, I will show you the characteristics of great growth shares and how to identify, value and select them and when to sell. I have repeated from *The Zulu Principle* some of the substance of the chapters on Competitive Advantage and Bull and Bear Markets. My thinking on these two topics is almost unchanged but I want this book to be self-contained. In all other respects, I have completely updated *The Zulu Principle* as far as growth shares are concerned.

I am confident that readers of this book will acquire a much better understanding of growth shares and, as a result, in the years ahead be able to select them better and beat the market by a significant margin.

SUMMARY

1. Private investors have three advantages that should help them beat the institutions:

    1) They have less money to invest, which means they can invest with more effect in smaller companies.

    2) Their first ten selections are usually sufficient to constitute their portfolio, whereas institutions are handicapped by having to invest in hundreds of shares.

    3) Their circle of competence can be more meaningfully applied to a small portfolio.

2. Joining an investment club is an excellent way for private investors to improve their knowledge of investment and widen their circle of competence. ProShare makes joining or forming an investment club very easy.

3. It pays to specialise and apply the Zulu Principle to investment. This book will concentrate exclusively on growth shares to help readers to become expert in selecting them.

4. Read as much as possible about investment. If you have not already done so, read one of the three best primers: *Beginner's Guide to Investment*, *How to Read the Financial Pages* or *Investment Made Easy*. All of them are available in paperback. I also suggest you read *The Zulu Principle*, or at least one other investment book of a similar standard.

5. *Company REFS* is the investment service I devised for active private investors. It is available daily on TOPIC, or monthly or quarterly in printed form. It gives a regular, reliable and comprehensive flow of the investment statistics that are essential for effective investment.

6. To make this book self-contained, some of the views I have expressed in *The Zulu Principle* will be repeated. Otherwise, it contains my most recent thinking on growth shares, and supersedes *The Zulu Principle* in that respect.

2

WHY GROWTH SHARES?

THE MAIN APPROACHES TO INVESTMENT

There are many different ways to invest. None is intrinsically better or worse than the others, but I would always recommend private investors to focus upon one main approach. That way they will learn more quickly and over the years become relatively expert in applying their chosen method.

There are three main approaches:

1. *Growth shares*

    Selecting shares with excellent growth prospects and benefiting from the compounding effect as their earnings per share (EPS) increase year after year.

2. *Asset situations*

    Buying shares in companies when their share prices have fallen below the underlying value of the business, as measured by its net asset value or, in more extreme cases, below its net current asset value.

3. *Technical analysis*

    Buying and selling shares on the basis of price movements, momentum and charts, irrespective of the financial fundamentals of the companies in question.

A distinction is often made between growth and value investment, where the term 'value' usually implies a discount to net assets. It is, however, a simplistic distinction. I consider myself to be a *growth* investor but my technique is essentially one of seeking out *value* within my chosen universe of growth shares. I simply measure value in a different way from traditional value investors. I will go into much more detail in later chapters about how I calculate the worth of a share. For now, suffice it to say that my approach sees value in a share if, for a comparable level of growth, it is rated on a lower price-earnings ratio (PER) than the other companies in its sector or the average of the market as a whole. All other things being equal, the lower a PER is relative to a company's growth rate, the more attractive I find the share.

The approach also provides a margin of safety, because if the market is not expecting much it will rarely be disappointed. Looking for value in growth shares provides a kind of investment 'double whammy': a short-term gain as the value anomaly is corrected and a long-term benefit from the compounding of earnings growth.

Investing in shares at a discount to their underlying net asset value can be a rewarding long-term policy. However, the results can be choppy as share price increases often depend on new management or takeovers, either of which may take several years to happen. Investing in asset situations can also be less tax-effective than investing in growth shares. Once a share price rises to the underlying value of a company's assets, most value investors take profits and move on to other stocks. As the profit is realised, a tax liability crystallises and has to be paid.

In contrast, excellent growth shares tend to be retained far longer than shares in asset situations. As a result, the tax liability on a growth share remains as a kind of interest-free loan from the Government while the share continues to be held. Tax considerations and the investment 'double whammy' are two good reasons to focus on growth shares, but there are others, such as the sheer scale of profits that can be achieved over many years. Take the example of one of the greatest growth shares ever.

THE COCA-COLA STORY

Coca-Cola was floated in 1919 at $40 per share, but within a year the price had dropped to $20 because of wild gyrations in the sugar price. Since then, we have been through the financial crashes of 1929, 1974 and 1987, a few major wars and a depression or two. In spite of all these vicissitudes, Coca-Cola has continued to grow remorselessly and, as a result, in early 1996 the original $40 investment, with income reinvested, was worth over $4m a share.

A REMARKABLE INVESTOR

Growth investors will also be encouraged by the story of Anne Scheiber who, after retiring from the US Internal Revenue Service, invested $5,000 in the stock market in 1944. When she died in 1995, at the age of 101, her $5,000 had grown to a fortune of $22m.

Anne Scheiber's broker says that she concentrated on leading growth stocks with great business franchises – companies like Coca-Cola and Schering-Plough. She did not deal very often, running her profits which compounded at an average rate of over 18% per annum.

In America, there is a much larger number of companies with great business franchises – a form of competitive advantage that I will elaborate upon in later chapters. The American home market is far bigger than that of the UK, and some of the American franchises, like McDonalds, Coca-Cola, Disney and Microsoft, are so strong that they are known all over the world. With companies like these, investors can take a very long-term view.

SOME UK EXAMPLES

In the UK, we are not so fortunate. Our home market is much smaller, so many of our domestic growth companies quickly reach saturation point. Nevertheless, a select number of UK companies have been real winners over the years. Rentokil, for example, has been a wonderful growth share; £10,000 invested in it 23 years ago would be worth £820,000 today. During the same period, £10,000 invested in Racal would have fared even better and would now be worth £1.5m, even disregarding the value of shares in Vodafone and Chubb that were given to Racal shareholders when those companies were spun off from their parent. In both cases, there would also have been a substantial and growing stream of dividends which, if reinvested, would have vastly increased the total returns.

If you failed to invest in Rentokil and Racal while they were in their infancy, you may feel that you have missed the boat. Do not despair – there are many other companies that are only beginning to show their paces. There is a good chance that a few of them will grow into the giants of the future.

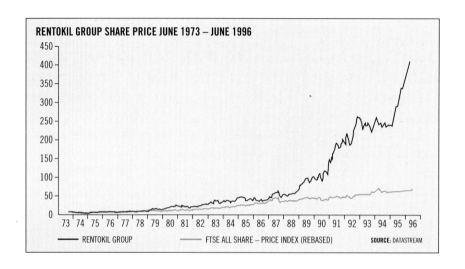

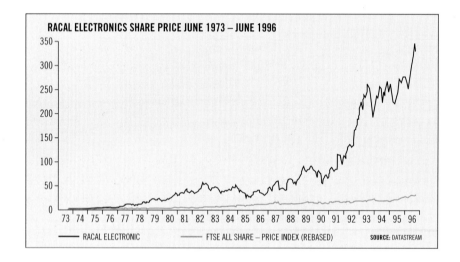

THE CASE FOR GROWTH SHARES

The story of Coca-Cola, the way Anne Scheiber built her fortune, and the UK examples of Rentokil and Racal show that the long-term gains of investing in growth shares can be enormous. Anne Scheiber's experience also illustrates the power of compounding money. Her average return of 18% per annum may not seem to be startling, but at that rate money doubles every four years, and over 40 it transformed $5,000 into a very sizeable fortune.

For all these reasons, I recommend growth shares as a staple investment diet. The upside potential is unlimited and, with a few precautions, the downside risk can also be minimised. This book is about growth shares and their wonderful potential, but the method of share selection I will show you has many influences. Technical analysis, fundamental measures such as cash flow, together with other important factors such as directors' buying, all add to the technique and make it a uniquely powerful approach to investment.

THE MARKET AS A WHOLE

The question I am most often asked at conferences is 'What do you think is going to happen to the stock market as a whole?' and I am always reminded of J. P. Morgan's answer to his liftboy. The young man had waited for a year or so to be alone in the lift with him. When the day came he asked the great man, 'Can you tell me what the market is likely to do today, Sir?' J. P. Morgan thought for a moment before delivering his verdict: 'It will fluctuate my boy, it will fluctuate.'

The short answer is that *nobody knows* if the market is about to go up or down. Bull markets climb a wall of worry so, by definition, investors are usually anxious while they are in progress. Conversely, bear markets usually strike when, as Joe Granville put it, 'The public is sleeping the slumber of confidence.'

There are usually a number of telltale signs of the market's likely future direction and I have devoted Chapter 14 to them. Meanwhile, remember that investment in growth shares is much more a matter of selection than timing.

SELECTION IS MORE IMPORTANT THAN TIMING

A couple of years ago, I read an interesting American study by CDA-Weisenberger which supports the argument for selection. It tracked the fortunes of two gifted men: Mr A who had the ability to time the market to perfection and Mr B who had always been fully invested in the best sectors. Both investors began with $1,000 on 31 March 1980 and by 30 September 1992, Mr A had been in and out of the market on nine occasions, timing each move to a nicety. His $1,000 had grown to $14,650.

However, Mr B, who had always been fully invested in the best sectors, turned his $1,000 into $62,640. During the same period, a $1,000 investment in the S & P 500 would have grown to a mere

$6,030. The results achieved by Mr A and Mr B would have been hard to emulate, but they do show clearly that selection is far more important than timing.

Since 1919, the UK stock market has beaten deposit interest by an average of more than 6% per annum. Most years, cash has been a depreciating asset, whereas the right growth shares have been appreciating assets that far more than offset the ravages of inflation. The main purpose of this book is to show private investors how to identify and select excellent growth shares and to ensure that they also know how to extract maximum profit from them by buying at attractive prices. Once investors become more confident about their powers of analysis in choosing shares, they also become much less worried about the state of the market at any particular moment.

SUMMARY

1. Growth shares are an excellent investment area to focus upon and apply the Zulu Principle of becoming *relatively* expert.

2. With the right selections, future capital gains, helped by the power of compounding, can be very substantial indeed.

3. A 'margin of safety' can be established by buying growth shares with low PERs in relation to their forecast EPS growth rates.

4. Running profits, with rare exceptions, makes good sense and is also a very tax-efficient policy.

5. Very little time should be spent worrying about the market as a whole. Investment is the art of the specific and selection is far more important than timing.

3

—

WHAT IS A GROWTH SHARE?

The word 'growth' is used to describe shares in companies which have the ability to increase earnings per share (EPS) at an above-average rate year after year. Although growing businesses frequently make acquisitions, it is the capacity to produce *organic growth from within* that is the distinguishing characteristic of great growth companies. EPS growth and share price growth are linked together like Tweedledum and Tweedledee.

Of course, growth shares have occasional setbacks in EPS as all companies are cyclical to some extent. The results of even the greatest growth companies are influenced by the state of the economy, but they are much less vulnerable than cyclical stocks.

One of the biggest single influences on the economy is the level and trend of interest rates. Highly cyclical stocks usually benefit when interest rates are falling as, in due course, this tends to stimulate the economy. Conversely, in difficult times when interest rates are rising, the profits of many cyclical stocks can be hit very badly. Growth shares are much better placed to shrug off short-term fluctuations in the economy.

THE RIGHT SECTORS

It follows that there are very few great growth companies in the most cyclical sectors, such as Building & Construction, Building Materials & Merchants, Paper, Packaging & Printing and Engineering. Vehicle distributors and steel producers are also at the sharp end of the economy and are usually among the first to suffer when interest rates rise. In some cases, they make such substantial losses during severe depressions that they have difficulty in surviving until the next boom.

My favourite sectors for finding growth stocks are Pharmaceuticals, Healthcare, Media, Support Services, Other Financial, Breweries, Pubs & Restaurants and General Retailers. The occasional growth share can be found outside these sectors, but they are very few and far between. Shares like Halma and Druck in Engineering, and First Technology in Engineering, Vehicles are exceptions that prove the rule.

Shipbuilders, automotive manufacturers and machine toolmakers may have been growth industries in the UK early this century, but they have now given way to sectors like Support Services, which contains many companies involved in the amazing growth of computer technology, and Media which has benefited so much from the explosive growth of television and the convergence of the previously separate technologies of computing and telecommunications. In Pharmaceuticals, investors are no longer interested in companies that make bicarbonate of soda; they are looking for businesses developing the products of the future – treatments for AIDS, hepatitis B, cancer or arthritis. Equally, a company making diaries is of very little interest when compared with a company like Psion, which makes the best palm-top computer of its kind.

Retailers are, of course, subject to cyclical influences, but some growth stocks in that sector still continue to perform even in the most difficult times. In many cases, this is because they have the capacity to *clone* their activities. Once they have established a successful formula for a shop or store they can roll it out across the country. While they are opening new branches, their EPS growth is usually exceptionally good. The worry comes when they reach saturation point. When this happens, they can be tempted to diversify or try the same formula abroad, where quite often it does not work so well.

It will not surprise you to see from the chart below that, in the long term, the industries of the future beat those that are highly cyclical. The chart shows the widely differing percentage performance of selected sectors during the last fifteen years.

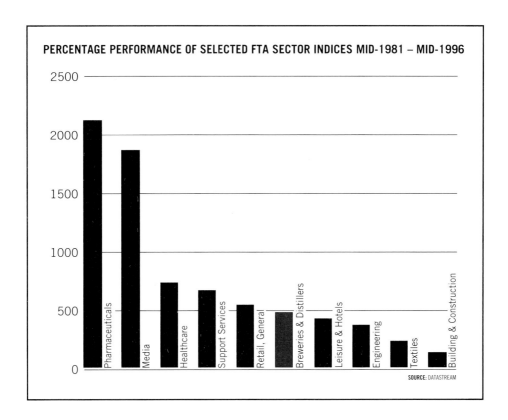

PERCENTAGE PERFORMANCE OF SELECTED FTA SECTOR INDICES MID-1981 – MID-1996

SOURCE: DATASTREAM

COMPETITIVE ADVANTAGE

There are other important reasons for the prevalence of great growth companies in strongly performing Pharmaceuticals and Healthcare. In many cases, these companies have a competitive advantage because they own patented drugs with international appeal. Other growth companies, like Marks & Spencer and Next, are protected by strong brand names and some, in television for example, are protected by Government franchises. The possession of a competitive advantage is a very important investment factor, so Chapter 9 is devoted to explaining it in much more detail. I do not want to dwell on competitive advantage at this stage because my approach is to check the hard arithmetic of a share before examining its less tangible qualities. If the PER, EPS growth and cash flow meet my criteria, I then make sure I can identify the competitive advantage responsible for the good figures – not the other way around.

Meanwhile, simply remember that being in the right kind of sector is a critical factor in deciding whether or not a business has the capacity to become a great growth stock.

MANAGEMENT

The calibre of management, and in particular of the chief executive, is obviously an important determinant of whether a good growth company can become a truly great one. Unfortunately, management ability is far more difficult to judge than past success in increasing EPS. Assessing the ability of other people is a skill possessed by very few of us and, as it is so easy to be misled, I prefer to rely more on the arithmetic. I will, however, review the problem of judging management in Chapter 8, because it is such an important element in making an investment decision.

EARNINGS PER SHARE GROWTH

To return to what can be measured and verified, the essence of a good growth stock is its capacity to increase EPS year after year. The first step in *finding* great growth stocks is to sieve the financial results of every company in the market, and especially those in the right sectors, to reduce the universe of shares in which you will make your search to those with a proven record of EPS growth and the expectation of more to come. Once that has been done, you are ready for the second step, which is to determine whether or not the price of the shares you have shortlisted is attractive or otherwise. Irrespective of a company's competitive advantage, and of its management capability, the first task is to see what the management has achieved to date and what brokers think it is likely to achieve during the next couple of years. This gives you an arithmetical fix on the company, which in turn will help to determine whether or not the shares are a possible buy.

At the beginning of 1996, the average forecast of EPS growth for the market as a whole was about 10%. In previous years, the average company has been forecast to grow at 12% per annum or a little more. It can therefore be assumed that a 15% rate of EPS growth is well above average and for that reason it is a sensible benchmark to insist upon as an absolute minimum. It is no mean achievement; over a five-year period, a 15% growth rate would double EPS.

COMPANY REFS' DEFINITION

When devising REFS, we had to decide upon the level of performance we would require from a company for it to qualify as a growth share. We knew that if we were too demanding, our sieves would eliminate some nascent growth companies and those that were likely to benefit from a recent management change. It is obviously vitally important to identify growth companies before all the action is over.

We decided that we would classify companies as growth companies if they had four years of consecutive EPS growth, *whether historic or forecast or a combination of the two*. In practice, this means that a company can just scrape in if it has two years of past EPS growth and two years of forecast future growth. In addition, however, there are a number of other criteria that need to be met:

1. Each of the past five years' results must have been profitable. None may show a loss.

2. Where four periods of growth follow a previous setback, it must have achieved, or be expected to achieve, its highest normalised EPS in the latest period out of the last six.

3. All companies in the Property sector are eliminated, because they are asset situations rather than growth companies.

4. There must be broker forecasts.

5. Companies in the highly cyclical Building & Construction and Building Materials & Merchants sectors and those in the Vehicle Distribution sub-sector are still required to meet the normal growth criteria. In addition, however, they are required not to have incurred a loss or suffered an EPS reversal in any of the last five years of reported results. This last criterion eliminates most of the companies in those sectors, but leaves the few that are arguably genuine growth companies.

It must be apparent from these criteria that REFS does not lightly classify companies as growth shares. In early 1996, about 50 companies in the FT-SE 100, 90 in the Mid-250 and 160 in the SmallCap indices made the grade. In these top three indices that constitute the FT-SE All-Share index, there are therefore about 300 REFS growth companies, less than half of the total, even after deducting the 125 investment trusts and 42 property companies from the 894 companies in the index. In the Fledgling index, excluding investment trusts, there are about 700 companies; REFS currently classifies only 60 of them as 'growth' companies. This is primarily due to the fact that the Fledgling index is made up of many demoted companies that have faltered. The index contains a large number of birds with broken wings as well as those that are learning to fly.

In devising REFS, we spent a great deal of time fine-tuning our definition of 'growth'. We wanted to ensure that only the most potentially rewarding shares qualified for the award of a crucially important investment measure, developed by me in the last three years and now a fundamental tool in my investment analysis. Called the price-earnings growth factor, or PEG for short, it is a measure of how the price of a share relates to its earnings growth rate. I will explain PEGs in detail in the next two chapters, but for now suffice it to say that only genuine growth companies are awarded PEGs.

Bear in mind that REFS does not take any account of the 15% limit for EPS growth that I referred to earlier. REFS is seeking to identify only those companies that have a four-year record of EPS growth, *even if they only just achieve it*. In REFS, a company would keep its growth classification by increasing its EPS annually by as little as 0.1%. It is therefore always advisable to study the five-year profits record in detail as sometimes a share might miss by a whisker the award of a PEG. In this kind of instance, if all of one's other investment criteria are fully met, it obviously makes sense to overlook the minor infraction of the REFS rules for awarding PEGs.

SUMMARY

1. Great growth companies have the ability to increase EPS at an above-average rate year after year.

2. Most growth companies are found in the 'new world' sectors of Support Services, Pharmaceuticals, Healthcare, Media, Electronic & Electrical Equipment, Breweries, Pubs & Restaurants and General Retailers.

3. Almost all companies are cyclical to some extent. However, companies in highly cyclical industries rarely become great growth companies.

4. A competitive advantage, such as a strong business franchise, patent or brand name, is often the main characteristic of great growth companies.

5. A company's capacity to clone an activity like a shop, restaurant, nursing home or indoor tennis facility, and open more of them throughout the country (and possibly internationally) can result in exceptional EPS growth.

6. Calibre of management is a crucial factor in deciding whether or not to buy a growth share, but it is very difficult to judge, so start with the arithmetic.

7. Try to find companies that are increasing EPS by at least 15% per annum. In a difficult year, a minor setback can be ignored, but 15% is the right average level to aim for – it will double EPS every five years.

8. The REFS definition of growth companies is set out in detail on page 27. In early 1996, about 50 companies in the FT-SE 100, 90 in the Mid-250 and 160 in the SmallCap made the grade. In the Fledgling there were only 60.

9. In REFS, only growth companies are awarded price-earnings growth factors (PEGs), a measure that I will explain fully in the next two chapters.

4

—

PRICE-EARNINGS
GROWTH FACTORS

The PER of a share is a measure of how much an investor is being asked to pay for future growth and how much (i.e. how many times EPS) other investors have paid in the past. It is far and away the most widely used measure of how cheap or expensive a growth share is despite the fact that it is only a one-dimensional measure. Far more meaningful, to my mind, is the relationship between the PER of a company and its expected rate of EPS growth. I call this the price-earnings growth factor – PEG for short. As far as I am aware, the PEG is the first attempt to analyse systematically this important relationship and I am convinced that it is an invaluable investment tool.

The PEG is calculated by dividing the prospective PER of a share by the estimated future growth rate in EPS. Say a company is growing at 12% per annum and has a prospective PER of 12, its PEG is $^{12}/_{12}$ = 1.0. If the growth rate were a much more attractive 24%, the PEG would be $^{12}/_{24}$ = 0.5, and if the growth rate were a relatively poor 6%, the PEG would be $^{12}/_{6}$ = 2.0.

Shares with PEGs of over one tend to be unappealing, shares with PEGs of about one are worthy of consideration and at well under one they are usually worth examining in much more detail with a view to purchase. In early 1996, the average PEG was about 1.5, having been nearer to 1.0 before the last bull market run. This historically high average PEG might be telling us that the bull market is nearing an end, but while I can find attractive stocks on PEGs of 0.75 or under, I am happy to continue investing in a highly selective way. However, I would not buy the market as a whole, because PEGs of 1.5 are too rich for my blood.

PEGs only apply to growth companies. The substantial EPS increases which are forecast by many cyclical companies are in most cases recoveries to previous levels or a step towards those levels.

Applying the PEG concept in relation to EPS increases of this kind would produce absurd and meaningless statistics.

The attraction of buying shares with low PEGs is that they provide the element of safety normally associated with low-risk investments without sacrificing the upside potential of growth stocks in their early stages. Take a share on a PEG of 0.5 with a PER of 12 and anticipated EPS growth of 24% per annum. Even if next year's profits disappoint a little, the share price is unlikely to fall much as the multiple is low and the shares are already very cheap in relation to the original forecast and the market as a whole.

The upside potential is far more interesting, even on the modest assumption that the forecast is just met. If EPS at the time of purchase were 10p and the shares at 120p were on a PER of 12, the expected 24% increase in earnings would lift EPS from 10p to 12.4p. Then, on a maintained PER of 12, the shares would rise by 24% to 148.8p (12 x 12.4p). However, it is extremely likely that the market would begin to wake up to the fact that the shares were undervalued. Investors would realise that the PER should be much higher and, in the weeks that followed the announcement of the results, the PER could easily improve to 18 times earnings and still leave the shares cheap relative to their growth rate.

On that basis, the shares would appreciate to 18 x 12.4p = 223.2p, a gain of 103.2p against the original purchase price of 120p. The interesting point is that only 28.8p (12 x 2.4p) of the profit of 103.2p arose from the increase in EPS, whereas 74.4p resulted from the *status change* in the PER. It is the possibility of a status change that investors should constantly be seeking when investing in companies with low PEGs.

Low PEGs work best when the PERs are in the 12–20 range and EPS growth rates are between 15% and 25%. Some of the best bargains are found amongst shares growing at about 25% per annum on a PER of 15, giving a PEG of 0.6. Exactly the same PEG would result from a growth rate of 50% and a PER of 30, but the important difference is that a growth rate of 50% is not sustainable in the longer term.

COMPARE CHALK WITH CHALK

The PEG factor is used as a calibrated measure to give an accurate fix on the comparative attractiveness of each company relative to both the market as a whole and other companies. It is an invaluable sieve for reducing the whole universe of growth shares to a small number of candidates for further sieving. The lower the PEG, the fewer the number of companies that will manage to get through the sieve.

For comparisons between PEGs to be meaningful, it is crucially important that the data from which they are calculated (the shares' PERs and growth rates) cover *exactly* the same period. It makes no sense to compare the growth statistics of a company with a March year end with another whose financial year ends three months earlier in December. Why? Because the business and economic world can change dramatically in a week, let alone three months. By adjusting the data for all companies to a common basis, comparisons are much more revealing and are always up to date and dynamic.

Think of it as the investment equivalent of a mother with an eighteen-month-old baby, Rosemary, and another with a nine-month-old one, Julie, comparing notes about their babies' progress. Rosemary's mother tells Julie's mother that Rosemary has just learned to recite a poem. The fact that nine-month-old Julie is unable to do so would not in any way imply that she is backward. The only way to compare the *relative* progress of the two babies is to check exactly what each of them is capable of at exactly the same age. The principle is just the same with companies: the period during which their results are being compared must be identical.

ROLLING TWELVE MONTHS AHEAD

To meet this important objective, REFS presents company statistics such as the dividend yield, PER, growth rate and PEG on a *rolling twelve months ahead basis*. To understand what this means, imagine a company, ABC, which has a December year end. Obviously, on 1 January 1996 the forecast that best describes ABC's prospects in the year ahead is the one for the year to 31 December 1996. Equally, on 1 January 1997 it is the forecast for the year to 31 December 1997. But how do you value the company on 1 March 1996? On that date, the year ahead is covered mainly by the 1996 forecast supplemented by a small part of the 1997 estimate. To be exact, it is $^{10}/_{12}$ of the 1996 figure and $^{2}/_{12}$ of that for 1997.

To see how this works in practice, consider these forecasts for ABC at a time when its shares are trading at 200p:

	EPS	PER	EPS GROWTH	PEG	DIV	YIELD
	p		%		p	%
Year to 31 December 1996	10	20.0	25*	0.80	5	3.13
Year to 31 December 1997	15	13.3	50	0.27	7	4.38

* Based on historic EPS of 8p for the year ended 31 December 1995.

On 1 March 1996, the forecast EPS for the following twelve months is calculated as follows:

$$(10p \times {}^{10}\!/_{12}) + (15p \times {}^{2}\!/_{12}) = 10.83p$$

The PER is calculated simply by dividing the share price of 200p by the rolling twelve months ahead EPS of 10.83p to give a twelve months ahead PER of 18.5.

The future EPS growth rate has to be calculated in two stages. First, it is necessary to establish as a base what EPS were for the twelve months *preceding* 1 March 1996. The calculation is made in this way:

$$(8p \times {}^{10}\!/_{12}) + (10p \times {}^{2}\!/_{12}) = 8.33p$$

The 8p in the first brackets is the historic EPS for the year ended 31 December 1995. For ten of the preceding twelve months this was the EPS base that was being improved upon. The 10p in the second brackets is the forecast EPS for 1996, which contains the two months needed to top up the ten in 1995 to cover a full twelve-month period *preceding* 1 March 1996.

The second stage is to calculate the precentage growth in EPS for the twelve months *following* 1 March 1996. Here is the calculation:

$$\frac{(10.83p - 8.33p)}{8.33p} \times 100 = +30\%$$

The rolling twelve months ahead PEG is calculated by dividing the prospective PER of 18.5 by the future growth rate of 30% to give 0.62.

The rolling twelve months ahead dividend is calculated in the same way as EPS: ${}^{10}\!/_{12}$ of the 5p for 1996 plus ${}^{2}\!/_{12}$ of the 7p for 1997, to give 5.33p.

To calculate the dividend yield, it is necessary to gross up the 5.33p dividend by adding back the ruling basic rate of tax – currently 20%. The resultant 6.66p is then divided by the share price of 200p to give a prospective yield of 3.33%.

The *rolling twelve months ahead* table then reads like this:

	EPS	PER	EPS GROWTH	PEG	DIV	YIELD
	p		%		p	%
Rolling 12 months ahead to 28 Feb. 97	10.83	18.5	30.0	0.62	5.33	3.33

Armed with these statistics, and only then, can a growth investor meaningfully compare ABC with another company, which has an end of February year end or has been brought, by making the same kind of calculations, onto a rolling twelve months ahead basis starting on 1 March. *The good news for REFS subscribers is that all of these calculations are made for them* and shown every month (daily on TOPIC) in the shaded panel of key statistics in the company entry. Three examples from the June 1996 issue are given overleaf:

GRANADA

PRICE (NMS 25) 3-JUN-96			**829p**
market cap			£7,027m
position			30th
index			FT-SE 100
norm eps (pr)			48.3p
turnover (95AR)			£2,381m
pretax (95AR)			£351m
			m s
DY (pr)	% 2.12		
PER (pr)	x 17.2		
PEG (pr)	f 0.91		
GR (pr)	% 18.9		
ROCE	% 34.0		
MARGIN	% 15.7		
GEAR	% 64.1		
PBV	x 15.1		
PTBV	x 15.1		
PCF	x 14.6		
PSR	x 2.03		
PRR	x na		
nav ps (95AR)			54.8p
net cash ps (95AR)			14.0p

ASDA

PRICE (NMS 200) 3-JUN-96			**118p**
market cap			£3,438m
position			60th
index			FT-SE 100
norm eps (pr)			8.26p
turnover (95AR)			£5,285m
pretax (95AR)			£257m
			m s
DY (pr)	% 3.18		
PER (pr)	x 14.2		
PEG (pr)	f 1.01		
GR (pr)	% 14.1		
ROCE	% 13.5		
MARGIN	% 4.75		
GEAR	% 28.4		
PBV	x 2.29		
PTBV	x 2.29		
PCF	x 10.3		
PSR	x 0.64		
PRR	x na		
nav ps (95AR)			51.4p
net cash ps (95AR)			na

MARKS & SPENCER

PRICE (NMS 50) 3-JUN-96			**462p**
market cap			£13,007m
position			10th
index			FT-SE 100
norm eps (pr)			26.9p
turnover (96PA)			£7,232m
pretax (96PA)			£966m
			m s
DY (pr)	% 3.44		
PER (pr)	x 17.2		
PEG (pr)	f 1.90		
GR (pr)	% 9.02		
ROCE	% 21.0		
MARGIN	% 13.1		
GEAR	% 1.74		
PBV	x 3.48		
PTBV	x 3.48		
PCF	x 19.4		
PSR	x 1.89		
PRR	x na		
nav ps (95AR)			133p
net cash ps (95AR)			16.5p

The black moons show how each company statistic compares with the market and sector averages – the blacker they are the better. The other key growth statistics will be explained more fully in Chapter 9.

There is another important advantage of using rolling twelve months ahead statistics. Fast-growing companies usually have high historic PERs, which can be very offputting to investors thinking in terms of the last financial year. Take, for example, a company that has grown at about 50% per annum compound and is forecast to continue doing so for the next few years. Its historic PER for the year ended 31 March 1996 could be about 30, which seems high in relation to the market as a whole. However, with further growth of 50%, the prospective PER for the year ending 31 March 1997 falls to 20 and for the year ending 31 March 1998 it drops to only 13.3. The REFS entry on 1 January 1997 would show the rolling PER for the twelve months immediately ahead, which would be calculated using ³⁄₁₂ of the PER for the year ending 31 March 1997 and ⁹⁄₁₂ of the PER for the year ending 31 March 1998. The REFS prospective PER would therefore be a much more attractive 15 times EPS and *obviously* a bargain in relation to a 50% growth rate, highlighted by a PEG of only 0.3.

The REFS approach enables investors to see clearly the kind of multiple they are really being asked to pay for such astonishing future growth. Also, every other company they compare it with will be portrayed on a similar basis. In REFS, chalk is always being compared with chalk.

There is no doubt that the rolling twelve months ahead basis helps to detect anomalous bargains very quickly, especially among companies with exceptional EPS growth rates. It is strange that no one else seems to work on forward statistics in quite the same way as REFS. In the many presentations I have given to private investors and to institutions, there has never been anything but praise for this approach. Everyone agrees that the idea is eminently sensible, so it has always surprised me that working with rolling twelve months ahead statistics has not become common practice. I suppose the reluctance of the institutions to change their ways should be welcomed. While big money continues to appraise companies using old methods, anomalies remain and, as a result, investment opportunities abound.

CHECKING THE VALIDITY OF FORECASTS

Comparing companies on the basis of their estimated future results is, of course, highly dependent on the accuracy of brokers' forecasts. The past few years' results may be historic, but at least they are factual, whereas forecasts are at best informed guesses. Sam Goldwyn, the American film magnate, put it very well: 'Forecasts are dangerous, particularly those about the future.'

The risk of being wrong about the consensus forecast can be lessened by taking a few elementary precautions. First, check the annual report and interim statement to find out *exactly* what the chairman has said about future prospects. Also, check press cuttings to see if anything has been added at the AGM or in interviews with the press. The REFS company entry always shows the last few price-sensitive forward-looking comments by the chairman starting from the most recent annual report. The tone and trend of them and of the newsflow is often just as important as the exact words that are used.

In their excellent book *Interpreting Company Reports and Accounts,* Geoffrey Holmes and Alan Sugden take an imaginary company, Polygon Holdings, in a range of industries and industrial climates and give their suggestions for estimating the year's profits based upon the chairman's comments on current trading:

Activity	Industrial climate	Chairman's remarks	Previous year £m	Reported year £m	Estimate of current year £m
Building	Continued recession	'Further decline inevitable'	1.0	0.8	0.5–0.6
Paper	Cyclical upturn	'Marked improvement'	2.2	1.8	2.4–2.8
Bookmaking	One of the UK's few growth industries	'Continued progress'	1.0	1.2	1.4–1.5
Plastic extrusions	Demand flat	'Market share increasing but lower margins'	0.6	0.75	0.6–0.8
Interest charges	Rates down 2%	'Improvement in liquidity likely'	–0.8	–1.0	–0.8
		Pre-tax total	4.0	3.55	4.1–4.9

The authors also draw attention to the necessity of keeping an eye open for any details of discontinued loss-makers (usually an excellent sign), of judging the chairman's previous record of forecasting (a helpful guide to this year's accuracy) and of being very wary of vague statements like: 'Unforeseen difficulties have occurred.'

Another useful indicator is the level of dividend paid and/or forecast. If dividends have been steadily rising and are then simply maintained, that can be a meaningful sign that there could be trouble ahead. Conversely, if the rate of increase in dividends is accelerated, it is obviously a bullish and confident gesture.

Further indicators can be of a more general nature. For example, the retail sales trends that are announced each month can be a useful pointer to the credibility of a retailer's forecast and so can the performance of competitors. You might notice in the press that the government of a foreign country has become disenchanted with the UK because the British Government failed to extradite someone or offended it in some other way. As a result, major contracts in the country in question might become more difficult to obtain by UK tenderers. Any UK company with a very substantial dependence on business in that country would be bound to suffer.

Like Eisenhower trying to judge the right place and time to invade

German-occupied Europe, you must take note of all the little signs and pieces of information you can put together. It is essential to monitor every share in your portfolio by keeping an eye on the validity of the brokers' consensus forecast that, more than anything else, underpins the share price.

BROKERS' CONSENSUS FORECASTS

Precise details of brokers' consensus details are shown in monthly publications like *The Estimate Directory*. They are now also shown in REFS each month as an essential part of the overall financial picture of a company.

Below is an extract from a typical REFS company entry, that of Medeva in June 1996:

BROKERS' CONSENSUS FORECASTS FOR MEDEVA JUNE 1996

Broker	Date	Rec	1996 ESTIMATES			1997 ESTIMATES		
			Pretax £m	Eps p	Dps p	Pretax £m	Eps p	Dps p
Daiwa Europe	31 Mar 95	ADD r	83.0 r	17.4 r	4.20 r			
Flemings	27 Jul 95	HOLD	95.0	18.7	4.60	105	21.8	5.10
Nikko Europe	17 Jan 96	HOLD −	96.8 +	19.7 −	4.60	104	21.4	5.00
BZW	20 Feb 96	BUY	90.4	19.5	4.50	106	22.9	5.27
UBS	20 Feb 96	BUY	90.0	18.5 +	4.80	100	20.5	5.50
Williams de Broe	28 Feb 96	BUY	90.0 −	19.2 −	4.50 −	100	20.3	5.00
Merrill Lynch	29 Feb 96	ACCU −	99.5 −	20.8 −	4.90 +	120	25.1	5.90
NatWest Securities	29 Feb 96	RED	94.0	19.6	4.70	103	21.3	5.10
Lehman Brothers	6 Mar 96	OUTP	89.9	18.8	4.60	102	21.4	
Panmure Gordon	15 Mar 96	BUY	95.0	19.7	4.50 −	110	22.8	5.00
HSBC James Capel	18 Mar 96	HOLD	95.0 +	19.2 +	4.80 +	103 −	20.1 −	5.50 +
SBC Warburg	21 Mar 96	HOLD	89.0 +	18.9 +	4.70 +	112 +	23.3 +	5.50 +
SGST	25 Mar 96	H/B	88.5 −	18.0 −	4.40 −	100	20.0	4.90
Salomon	9 Apr 96	HOLD	94.0	18.8	4.70	115	22.0	5.40
Credit Lyonnais Laing	11 Apr 96	BUY	94.0	19.0	4.80	103	20.8	5.50
Greig Middleton	15 Apr 96	BUY	88.0 −	18.4 −	4.50 −	97.0	20.2	5.10
	Consensus	WBUY	92.4	19.2	4.59	103	21.1	5.27
	1M Change		+0.09	+0.08	−0.05	−2.21	−0.41	−0.01
	3M Change		−1.74	−0.42	−0.29	−3.21	−0.80	−0.06

A number of points deserve special attention when studying details of the brokers' consensus forecast:

1. The reliability of the consensus forecast (and therefore of the PEG) is obviously enhanced if there are a large number of brokers (say five or more) covering the company with a small standard deviation from the average forecast. The sixteen brokers' estimates for Medeva provide a substantial degree of comfort. Watch out for the lemming effect, however. If a prestigious and top-notch broker makes a forecast for a company in an industry in which he is known to specialise, it is very tempting for an analyst working for a lesser firm to take a lead from the much more detailed research.

2. The company's own broker or brokers are highlighted in a panel above the Outlook statement. I pay special attention to the company brokers' forecasts especially if, as in the case of Medeva, the brokers in question are as prestigious as BZW and Panmure Gordon. The company broker should be better informed and is less likely to take the risk of embarrassing the company with over-optimistic forecasts.

3. The dates of brokers' forecasts are of critical importance. Forecasts are excluded if they have been overtaken by events, actual results or a profit warning. The remaining forecasts are weighted for age when calculating the consensus.

4. The Buy, Hold, Sell, Outperform, Add, Accumulate and Reduce recommendations of all of the brokers give a fair idea of the popularity of a share. As you can see, the consensus for Medeva is W Buy, which stands for Weak Buy. The full range of how individual recommendations are expressed in REFS as a consensus is as follows:

Strong Buy	Weak Buy/Hold	Weak Sell
Buy	Hold	Sell
Weak Buy	Weak Sell/Hold	Strong Sell

5. The plus or minus signs indicate if the particular element of the forecast was upgraded or downgraded compared with the previous

forecast. If there is no sign, that element of the forecast either remained the same or is a completely new forecast.

6. The one-month overall change and three-month overall change are shown at the bottom of the page. A keen eye should be kept on these figures as they can indicate if newsflow is remaining positive or beginning to turn negative.

7. An important caveat about the EPS figures is that the tax rate sometimes varies substantially. When a company is recovering from a loss-making position, after a year or so any tax losses brought forward are likely to be exhausted. At this point, the company begins to pay a full tax charge again and EPS are reduced accordingly. Even though profits before tax per share might be increasing by, say, 20% in the year ahead, this could be masked by the increased tax charge. It therefore pays to keep an eye on pre-tax profits figures as well as EPS and to double-check the historic and forecast tax rates which are shown in the panel of seven-year figures.

Brokers are often slow to update their forecasts, so always keep an eye on the relative strength of the share price against the market. It is often an early indicator that a company's situation is changing for the better or worse. This subject is dealt with much more fully in Chapter 7 on Relative Strength and Chapter 15 on Portfolio Management.

There is always a risk that the brokers' consensus forecast will not be met. However, by studying the detailed brokers' forecasts and their recommendations set out in REFS, reading the chairman's comments and press announcements and noting articles about general conditions in the industry, you can reduce the risk to an acceptable level.

SUMMARY

1. The PER is a one-dimensional measure. Far more meaningful is the PEG which shows the relationship between the PER of a company and its expected rate of EPS growth.

2. The PEG is calculated by dividing the prospective PER of a company by its estimated future growth rate in EPS. Both the

prospective PER and the growth rate should be calculated on a rolling twelve months ahead basis.

3. The average PEG in the market in early 1996 was about 1.5. PEGs of over 1.5 are unattractive, not very attractive between 1.0 and 1.5 and of great interest well below 1.0.

4. REFS awards PEGs only to growth companies which have at least four years of consecutive growth whether it be historic or forecast or a combination of the two. They must also meet a number of other criteria set out in Chapter 3 on page 27.

5. Low PEGs work best in the 12–20 range of PERs with substantial annual growth rates in EPS of between 15% and 30%.

6. Shares with low PEGs combine aggressiveness with a safety factor. The aggression comes from the likelihood of an upward status change in the PER, which often has a greater impact on the share price than the increase in EPS. The safety comes from the capacity of shares with low PEGs to handle minor disappointments in actual EPS growth rates against consensus forecasts. If, for example, the EPS growth of a company turned out to be only 20% instead of an anticipated 25%, the shares would still be relatively cheap if they were on a prospective multiple of, say, 15.

7. Growth stocks can only be compared with each other when they are first reduced to a like-for-like basis. Expressing their growth statistics (PERs, PEGs, growth rates and dividend yields) on a rolling twelve months ahead basis achieves this objective and has the added attraction of being up to date and dynamic.

8. To lessen the risk of brokers' forecasts misleading you, double-check the annual report and interim statement to find out exactly what has been said by the chairman about future prospects. Also check press cuttings and the news flow in the REFS company entry.

   Other indicators include the level of dividends and the general trend of sales in the industry as a whole, especially with retailing companies, and any other major developments that could have a particularly adverse or beneficial effect on the company in question.

9. Whenever possible, also check the individual brokers' forecasts that constitute the brokers' consensus forecasts. These are available in REFS or *The Estimate Directory*.

    Draw comfort from a large number of brokers forecasting with a smallish standard deviation from the average forecast. Pay particular attention to the company's broker's forecast and to more recent forecasts.

    Watch the trend of revisions to forecasts, especially if newsflow begins to deteriorate.

10. Always note the tax charge for each year. Sometimes a rising tax charge can obscure real growth, as it reduces EPS for a particular year.

5

—

PEGS AT WORK

PEG TESTS

We have been producing REFS long enough now to see how low PEGs have worked in practice as an investment measure. The table below shows the results of eight periods of six months ended 30 September 1995 through to 30 April 1996:

How shares with PEGs of under 0.6 have consistently beaten the market				
Six months ended 30.9.95				
FT-SE Index	Market Performance	Low PEG Performance	No. of Qualifying Companies	Low PEG Outperformance %
FT-SE 100	12.0	20.0	3	66.7
Mid 250	15.2	12.4	13	-18.6
SmallCap	14.9	29.7	25	99.1
All-Share	13.0	23.5	41	80.8
Six months ended 31.10.95				
FT-SE 100	8.8	13.7	6	55.3
Mid 250	10.0	8.8	13	-11.9
SmallCap	10.2	28.9	23	183.1
All-Share	9.1	20.5	42	125.3
Six months ended 30.11.95				
FT-SE 100	9.6	17.2	7	78.8
Mid 250	8.3	18.3	12	121.0
SmallCap	5.2	27.5	19	428.8
All-Share	9.0	22.7	38	152.2

How shares with PEGs of under 0.6 have consistently beaten the market (cont.)				
Six months ended 31.12.95				
FT-SE Index	Market Performance	Low PEG Performance	No. of Qualifying Companies	Low PEG Outperformance %
FT-SE 100	11.3	23.6	3	108.5
Mid 250	12.1	20.2	15	67.1
SmallCap	5.7	32.0	25	458.5
All-Share	11.0	27.3	43	147.4
Six months ended 30.1.96				
FT-SE 100	7.2	28.9	1	299.4
Mid 250	5.9	10.0	9	69.3
SmallCap	3.9	21.5	23	446.1
All-Share	6.7	18.6	33	176.8
Six months ended 29.2.96				
FT-SE 100	5.1	30.4	2	498.0
Mid 250	7.3	5.5	6	-24.0
SmallCap	4.4	14.6	19	234.5
All-Share	5.5	13.7	27	151.7
Six months ended 31.3.96				
FT-SE 100	5.6	29.2	2	419.2
Mid 250	9.3	10.1	4	8.9
SmallCap	6.4	33.2	13	419.6
All-Share	6.4	27.9	19	335.8
Six months ended 30.4.96				
FT-SE 100	8.5	31.3	2	267.3
Mid 250	18.3	16.5	3	-9.9
SmallCap	15.0	22.4	18	49.4
All-Share	10.7	29.2	23	172.7

As you can see, the shares with PEGs of under 0.6 beat the market by a wide margin in each six-month period. They averaged a 22.9% rise compared with just 8.9% for the market as a whole. In other words, low PEG shares rose 2.5 times as much as the market.

We used a period of six months for each test as it usually takes that long for the status change in the PER to work its way through into the share price. Also, a six-month period embraces either the annual or interim results, giving the company and its shares an important moment in the spotlight. After the six months, the process can be repeated to catch the next candidates for a status change. Some shares from the first list will, of course, still justify a place on many future lists.

Fledgling index shares are excluded from the tests because most of the consensus forecasts are supported by only one broker's estimate and many of the shares are relatively unmarketable. This does not mean that investors should avoid the Fledgling index, but they should treat it with caution.

The word 'Fledgling' suggests a young company about to fly. In the case of companies like Azlan Group and Pressac Holdings, this was undoubtedly the case. However, it should be borne in mind that the Fledgling index is also a receptacle for companies that have fallen out of the FT-SE SmallCap index and those above it. In other words, as well as being a birthplace, it is also a kind of graveyard.

The ideal hunting grounds for shares with low PEGs and very attractive prospects are the FT-SE SmallCap index and non-index companies, which include new issues that often offer great opportunities. One of my recent favourites, JJB Sports, is a good example. It was floated in November 1994 at 215p and by the end of 1995 stood at 620p.* In January 1996, it announced that like-for-like sales were up 18%, overall sales were up over 50% and margins had improved slightly. Even after such a sensational rise, the shares appeared to have plenty of steam left in them.

The PEG principle also works exceptionally well with shares in the highly marketable FT-SE 100 and Mid-250 indices. REFS provides league tables of companies with the lowest PEGs in each of the indices, from the FT-SE 100 down to the AIM. For example, Forte at 248p was top of the October 1995 FT-SE 100 table with a PEG of only 0.52 prior to the bid by Granada. The performance of low PEG companies in the top two indices is evidenced by the tables below, covering thirteen periods of six months; the first ended on 30 April 1995 and the last on 30 April 1996. As you can see, non-cyclicals with PEGs of 0.75 or under outperformed the two main indices substantially. We lifted the

---

* This was before a 2 for 1 issue in mid-1996.

PEG cut-off from 0.6 to 0.75 because the shares in the two top indices are far more marketable. They are, therefore, more popular with institutions and higher market ratings are to be expected.

During the six-month tests, the FT-SE 100 index rose by an average of only 9.53%, whereas the low PEG stocks rose by 21.04% and the Mid-250 rose by an average of 9.56% against 14.88% for the low PEG stocks.

PEG PERFORMANCE COMPARISONS
FT-SE 100 index growth companies with PEGs of less than 0.75

Six Months Ended	Number of Companies	Index Growth %	Low PEGs Performance %	Low PEG Outperformance %
APR 30 1995	4	6.39	10.89	70.42
MAY 31 1995	6	9.23	7.54	-18.31
JUNE 30 1995	5	8.12	6.31	-22.29
JULY 31 1995	7	15.26	25.79	69.00
AUG 31 1995	6	16.51	26.69	61.66
SEPT 30 1995	3	12.18	17.74	45.65
OCT 31 1995	4	8.79	21.83	148.35
NOV 30 1995	7	9.64	24.46	153.73
DEC 31 1995	7	11.30	26.85	137.61
JAN 31 1996	4	7.21	28.03	288.77
FEB 29 1996	3	5.09	24.93	389.78
MAR 31 1996	2	5.63	29.23	419.18
APR 30 1996	3	8.52	23.25	172.89
AVERAGE	**5**	**9.53**	**21.04**	**147.42**

PEG PERFORMANCE COMPARISONS
FT-SE 250 Midcap index growth companies with PEGs of less than 0.75

Six Months Ended	Number of Companies	Index Growth %	Low PEGs Performance %	Low PEG Outperformance %
APR 30 1995	20	0.83	1.41	69.88
MAY 31 1995	17	4.36	5.21	19.50
JUNE 30 1995	20	2.80	8.55	205.36
JULY 31 1995	22	14.41	11.97	-16.93
AUG 31 1995	22	15.53	20.44	31.62
SEP 30 1995	24	15.16	14.73	-2.84
OCT 31 1995	22	10.01	12.25	22.38
NOV 30 1995	18	8.30	15.75	89.76
DEC 31 1995	20	12.08	16.61	37.50
JAN 31 1996	20	5.90	11.04	87.12
FEB 29 1996	19	7.29	27.07	271.33
MAR 31 1996	13	9.30	23.98	157.85
APR 30 1996	16	18.28	24.43	33.64
AVERAGE	**19**	**9.56**	**14.88**	**77.40**

The interesting and satisfying point to note is that when the low PEG approach failed, the loss against the market was negligible. In the FT-SE 100, the *worst* period was the six months ended 30 June 1995, when the index rose by 8.12% and its low PEG shares only rose by 6.31%. In the best periods, however, the outperformance was massive. For example, during the six months ended 29 February 1996, the FT-SE 100 index rose by 5.09%, while the low PEG shares dwarfed this with a rise of nearly 25%. In the Mid-250 the results were not quite so impressive, but the pattern was similar.

Many people have been surprised by these excellent results. I am surprised that they are surprised. If the market in early 1996 was on a prospective PER of 15 and was looking forward to only 10% EPS growth in the year ahead, the average PEG was a lofty 1.5. It seems obvious to me that companies with average PERs of 15, but with future growth rates of 20% and PEGs of 0.75, should outperform the market. It would be very strange if they did not do so.

I am sure you will agree my system already gives you an exciting edge, but read on before you rush out and put it into practice. I will take the argument a stage further in later chapters, and by introducing additional sieves show you how to improve performance still further.

The test results shown in the tables are still far from conclusive. They represent all that we have had time to test at the time of writing this book. The tests will be on-going and the comparative results will be calculated every month. There are bound to be times when shares with low PEGs do not fare so well as the market or a particular index.

A possible danger period for low PEG shares might be near to the end of a bull market. Great growth shares would have beaten the market on the way up and be near to their all-time highs. When the bear strikes, investors often panic and snatch profits, on shares that have done well, before they disappear. It will not surprise me therefore if, for brief periods in a bear market, shares with low PEGs are a little disappointing. However, investment is a business of averages and I remain very confident that, on balance, it makes absolute sense to invest in growth companies that are growing faster than their contemporaries, satisfy a number of highly selective criteria and are on cheaper multiples in relation to their growth rates.

AVOID SHARES ON VERY HIGH PERS

There is an old maxim that, at some future time, exceptional growth rates regress to the norm. The logic is obvious; if a company grew at, say, 50% per annum for a 20-year period, it would be over 3,000 times bigger than when it started. If the company then carried on growing at the same rate, it would not be long before it owned the world.

On the way, the company would attract vigorous international competition. There would also be the risk of substitutes being introduced for its products or services. The business would almost certainly become unwieldy and, from time to time, management might become complacent. One way or another, market forces would combine to bring down the company's exceptional growth rate.

Any company on a very high PER is living on borrowed time as far as its market rating is concerned. Sooner or later, the growth rate will slacken and the PER will fall to a more normal level and then to an average level or even below it.

In the UK, Hanson has been a good example of this transition. There is no doubt that, during its long heyday, it was brilliantly managed. As the company climbed the ladder to become one of the UK's ten biggest companies, Lord Hanson and the late Lord White grew older and had less to prove. The company began to settle down and grow at a more normal pace. The attempt to take over ICI can now be seen as a kind of last fling of the old guard. During the last three decades, the PER has fallen from as much as 25 times earnings in the best years in the sixties and seventies to the 1996 prospective level of only 10 times earnings with the shares standing at a substantial discount to the market average. There is nothing abnormal in this – it is a natural process. A very similar thing happened to Xerox, which was a great growth stock with a PER in its early days of over 100. Xerox fulfilled most of its early promise and today the company is a giant with an average PER and an average growth rate.

A share with a very high growth rate of, say, 50% must be assumed to be close to the point at which this process of regression will start. In a sense, therefore, the investor needs to amortise a proportion of the likely regression every year. A growth rate of 50% per annum is wonderful while it lasts, but the most I am prepared to pay for any growth share is 20 times *prospective* earnings. In fact, I prefer a lower growth rate of, say, 30% with a prospective PER of about 15 which, as it happens, was the market average at the beginning of 1996. I know that 15 is an undemanding level for a PER if growth is maintained, and 30% is obviously far easier to sustain than 50%. Even if the 30% growth rate slackens to 20% and over a very long period to 15%, the PER of 15 would probably hold at about that level. It is a great comfort to know that there should be very little erosion in the PER, if all goes reasonably well for the company. With sky-high multiples, an investor always needs to be on red alert waiting for the slightest slackening of the extraordinary growth rates that justify them. Remember that the large upward movement in a share price caused by a status change in a company's PER can go into reverse. A relatively minor setback can easily cause an astronomic PER to crumble.

SUMMARY

1. REFS tests of shares with low PEGs during 1995/6 have shown very encouraging results. On average during eight tests of six-monthly periods, the increase achieved by the market was only 9%, whereas shares with PEGs of under 0.6 rose by an average of almost 23% – 2.5 times the market. Thirteen further six-month tests showed that companies with PEGs of 0.75 or under in the FT-SE 100 and Mid-250 very substantially outperformed their respective indices.

2. The Fledgling index contains very few shares with PEGs as in addition to being a launching pad for new young companies, it is also a dustbin for tired old ones. Investors should also be wary of PEGs based on only one broker's forecast and wary of the marketability of Fledgling companies.

3. Shares with prospective PERs of over 20 are more vulnerable in a bear market. Eventually the high PER (and the high EPS growth that justifies it) will regress to the norm. The shares may have to work hard to stand still, so shares with excessive multiples should be avoided.

6

—

CASH FLOW

Generalising about investment can be dangerous but I can tell you with confidence that shares with excellent cash flow are invariably attractive. The converse is also true – companies which fail to turn their profits into cash are suspect.

There is no more reassuring investment than a good growth share with healthy cash balances and cash flow per share well in excess of EPS. Cash flow is far more difficult to fudge than earnings and for that reason an abundance of it helps to provide a measure of protection against creative accounting, which has been the downfall of many seemingly attractive growth shares.

Many American investors look upon cash flow as the single most important factor in appraising a company. Warren Buffett put it succinctly when he said, 'Not all earnings are created equal.' The distinction he draws is between companies that generate surplus cash, which can be distributed to shareholders as dividends or spent on genuine expansion, and those that need to spend most of their profits on new and replacement plant and machinery *just to stay in business*.

To establish a company's cash flow, you need to add back to profits items like depreciation, which require no cash outlay. The Accounting Standards Board has a mandatory requirement for a Cash Flow Statement, which splits cash flow into different categories and attempts to classify movements by their economic causes. Headings now include Net Cash Inflow from Operating Activities and, under FRS1,* this figure must be reconciled with operating profits. Other than depreciation and associated company profits, the main additional items are increases and decreases in working capital (i.e. stocks, debtors and creditors). A typical reconciliation might be as follows:

---

* In accordance with their policy of regularly reviewing all accounting standards, the ASB has published proposals to revise FRS1. If accepted, these proposals will further enhance the value of data provided in this key financial statement.

		£000
Operating profit		1000
Depreciation		100
Increase in stocks		(10)
Increase in creditors		50
Decrease in debtors		40
NET CASH INFLOW FROM OPERATING ACTIVITIES		1180
RETURNS ON INVESTMENTS AND SERVICING OF FINANCE		
Interest Received	100	
Interest paid	(250)	
Interest element of finance lease rentals payment	(40)	
Dividends received from associated undertaking	60	
Dividends paid (excluding ordinary dividends)	(20)	
NET CASH OUTFLOW FROM RETURNS ON INVESTMENTS AND SERVICING OF FINANCE		(150)
TAXATION		
UK corporation tax paid	250	
Overseas tax paid	30	
		(280)
NET CASH FLOW		750

The price-to-cash flow (PCF) of a company is calculated by dividing a company's market capitalisation by its cash flow. In the example given, if the market capitalisation was £15m, this would mean that the PCF was $\dfrac{£15m}{£750,000} = 20$

It is important to realise that the PCF does not indicate in itself if a company has a strong cash flow; it simply tells you the number of times cash flow per share you have to pay to buy shares in the company (i.e. whether the shares are cheap or dear in relation to cash flow).

Healthy cash flow is needed to fund the following:

1. Repayment of any loans

2. Future capital expenditure

3. Dividends on ordinary shares

4. Buying back ordinary shares in the market. (This can be very good news for investors, as it enhances EPS and it tightens the supply of the company's shares, putting upward pressure on the price).

ADVANTAGES OF STRONG CASH FLOW

Cash flow is the life blood of any business. In addition to providing a check on creative accounting, it also highlights:

a) If the future dividend is safe.

b) The probable trend of liquidity and gearing. Cash flow is the raw material from which debts can be paid off and liquidity improved. Unless cash flow is strong, gearing will increase and liquidity will deteriorate.

c) If a company has been over-trading. When earnings per share are expanding rapidly and cash flow is shrinking, this can indicate over-trading; for example, excessive funds may be locked up in growing stocks and debtors. This, in turn, raises the question of whether credit policy is too lax or if customers are unable to pay.

d) If future expansion plans and proposed future capital expenditure can be funded from within.

CONSTRUCTING A CASH FLOW SIEVE

To construct a sieve based on cash flow per share, it is necessary to relate it to EPS for the same accounting period. An undemanding sieve, that works well in practice, is simply to require cash flow to be in excess of EPS per share for the last reported year and for the five-year average. A good broker should be able to give you the necessary details and REFS also provides the answer every month. As you can see from the panel taken from the May 1996 company entry of JJB Sports, in 1992 cash flow per share was only 1.93p against normalised EPS of 5.53p. In later years the shortfall was rectified and in 1995, for example, cash flow per share of 21.4p exceeded EPS of 19.4p. Capital expenditure was also well covered by cash flow.

JJB SPORTS

year ended 31 Jan		1992	1993	1994	1995	1996P	1997E	1998E
turnover	£m	29.1	34.3	43.8	61.3	89.6		
depreciation	£m	0.76	0.86	0.98	1.16			
int paid (net)	£m	0.20	0.23	0.10	-0.15			
FRS3 pretax	£m	2.18	2.92	4.58	7.59	12.9		
norm pretax	£m	2.20	2.93	4.62	7.75		17.5	20.0
turnover ps	£	1.16	1.37	1.75	2.35			
op margin	%	8.24	9.22	10.8	12.4			
ROCE	%	44.6	37.1	46.4	34.8			
ROE	%	23.8	25.1	32.9	22.6			
FRS3 eps	p	5.48	7.35	12.4	18.8	27.7		
IIMR eps	p	5.53	7.39	12.6	19.4			
norm eps	p	5.53	7.39	12.6	19.4	27.7	37.4	42.7
norm eps growth	%		+33.6	+70.1	+53.9	+43.4	+34.9	+14.1
tax rate	%	37	37	32	36		35	35
norm per	x					27.2	20.2	17.7
cash flow ps	p	1.93	11.6	16.2	21.4			
capex ps	p	8.46	5.12	7.90	7.91			
dividend ps	p	–	–	–	3.22	8.75	11.0	14.0
dps growth	%					+172	+25.7	+27.3
dividend yield	%					1.45	1.82	2.32
dividend cover	x				6.01	3.17	3.40	3.05
shrholders funds	£m	5.23	6.74	9.03	21.6			
net borrowings	£m	-0.01	1.18	-0.17	-11.9			
net curr assets	£m	0.51	1.48	2.68	14.6			
ntav ps	p	19.2	25.3	34.5	71.9			

With an *exceptional* growth share, it would not be unduly worrisome if for one year only cash flow per share was *slightly* less than EPS provided that the cash flow statement and tone of the chairman's statement made it abundantly clear that the cause was increased debtors and/or stocks to finance expansion. If, however, the five-year average of cash flow was also lower than the five-year average of EPS, that would put me off. Ideally, cash flow per share for the last reported year and for the five-year average should be in excess of EPS. This is a simple and reassuring sieve. Of course, there will be the odd growth share that has poor cash flow for very good reason and performs exceptionally well. But investment is essentially a game of averages and the security the cash flow sieve gives me more than outweighs the annoyance of missing the occasional winner.

As you can see from the figures below, the cash flow filter had a varying effect on the performance of shares with PEGs below 0.6 that were tested against the market in Chapter 5:

Six months ended	All-Share Index %	Performance of PEGs below 0.6 %	+ Cash Flow Filter %
30 September 1995	13.0	23.5	26.3
31 October 1995	9.1	20.5	20.3
30 November 1995	9.0	22.7	20.4
31 December 1995	11.0	27.3	24.5
31 January 1996	6.7	18.6	18.1
29 February 1996	5.5	13.7	14.9
31 March 1996	6.4	27.9	14.9
30 April 1996	10.7	29.2	33.6
AVERAGE GAIN	8.9	22.9	21.6

Overall, the results were slightly disappointing as they had little or no impact on performance. I stand by the sieve, however, as it makes me feel much more comfortable, especially with SmallCap and Fledgling shares. I also anticipate that the cash flow sieve will be at its most effective in a bear market.

Some interesting evidence of the attractions of strong cash flow per share came from an earlier test covering the six months ended 30 September 1995. REFS analysed the whole of the FT-SE SmallCap table of companies with the lowest PEGs, comprising 55 shares ranging from PEGs of 0.32 to 0.83. In spite of there being no cut-off for the PEGs, on average the shares outperformed the market by about 50% and 51 of the 55 shares made money. The interesting point is that when the cash flow sieve was applied, although it eliminated a few winners, it also knocked out three of the four losers.

The requirement of cash flow per share to at least exceed EPS is a very slender one. To be more demanding, investors could insist upon, say, 1.5 times cover when constructing their sieve. The advantage of one times cover is that it is simple and seems to work reasonably well. I therefore recommend it and suggest that if a company's cash flow per share is *much* better than its EPS, this should be held in its favour in the final weighing up of whether or not its shares are a buy.

CAPITAL EXPENDITURE

Capital expenditure is a use of cash flow rather than a charge against it. However, in some cases, capital expenditure is necessary for the continuance of a business (e.g. the replacement of old machines with new ones for exactly the same purpose).

Capital expenditure on brand new machines for a new and additional factory is quite another matter. Unfortunately, it is not possible to distinguish readily between capital expenditure on expansion and on necessary replacement. Investors should, however, keep an eye on the level of capital expenditure each year and try to determine from broker and press comment how much of it is expansionary and how much is mandatory.

In REFS, we exclude property from our capital expenditure per share statistics, as money spent on property is *usually* expansionary and is almost always discretionary (as property can be leased). This is, of course, a very arbitrary assessment, but it does seem to work quite well and highlights some interesting anomalies. For example, over the five years ending 1994/5 the water companies have used most of their cash flow on capital expenditure. In contrast, the electricity companies have spent on capital account an average of about 50%.

There are companies (usually in engineering of some kind) that *must* spend vast sums on new or replacement plant and machinery just to stay alive. There are others, in retailing for example, that spit out cash and have very little demand for capital expenditure.

Companies that eat shareholders' cash might well be called 'cash-guzzlers'. In my experience they are rarely investor-friendly, so avoid companies with capital expenditure over the last five years that exceeds their cash flow. Look for companies with cash flow well in excess of capital expenditure, with a view to ensuring that something worthwhile will be left over for shareholders.

OWNERS' EARNINGS

A reader of *The Zulu Principle* wrote to me in June 1995 suggesting that a more meaningful investment measure than a price-earnings ratio might be a price-to-owners'-earnings ratio (POER). Say, for example, that you had the choice of investing in two companies, both of which had just reported EPS of 50p per share and cash flow per share of 100p. If company A was a cash-guzzler and had to spend 70p per share per annum on capital expenditure just to stay in business and company B needed to spend only 30p, company B would obviously be much more attractive to shareholders. With company A, the cash-guzzler, 'owners' earnings' (cash flow less capital expenditure – but see footnote) would be only 30p per share (100p minus 70p) but, with company B, it would be 2.3 times as much at 70p (100p minus 30p). Those precious owners' earnings are needed to provide the cash for increasing dividends, repaying debt and for genuine expansion.

From just one year's accounts, it is impossible to judge whether or not a company spends most of its cash flow on capital items. The five-year figures should be examined to establish the long-term relationship between EPS and cash flow and the proportion of cash flow that is likely to be needed for capital expenditure.

Say that both company A and company B are projecting future growth in EPS of 20% and that they are both currently quoted at £6 a share. Next year's EPS will grow from 50p to 60p, so both companies' prospective PERs are 10. Their PEGs are also very attractive at 0.5 (10 divided by 20). It is only when the POERs are calculated that the difference between the two becomes apparent.

Assume that both companies' cash flow is usually about double their EPS, and that company A normally spends about 70% of its available cash flow on capital expenditure, in contrast to company B which spends an average of only 30%. The two companies can be compared as follows:

---

*Warren Buffett calculates owners' earnings by adding depreciation, depletion and amortisation charges to net income. He then deducts the capital expenditure a company is likely to need together with any additional working capital that might be required to maintain its economic position and unit volume. Taking REFS' five-year cash flow per share figures and deducting capex gets close enough to Buffett's calculation in a quick rule-of-thumb way.

	Company A	Company B
	p	p
Prospective EPS	60	60
Cash flow per share	120	120
Less Capex	84	36
Owners' earnings	36	84
Share price	600	600
POER	16.6	7.1

The relative POERs of company A and company B are startling enough to establish that company B is the more attractive of the two by a wide margin. The reader who wrote to me also suggested that it might be possible to go further and calculate a POER growth factor, similar to a PEG. Keep an eye on REFS, we might take this further.

SUMMARY

1. Cash flow is more difficult to fudge than earnings.

2. A low PCF does not in itself indicate that a company has strong cash flow. The PCF simply tells you whether the shares are cheap or dear in relation to cash flow.

3. A healthy cash flow is needed to fund the following:

   1. Repayment of loans

   2. Future capital expenditure

   3. Dividends on ordinary shares

   4. Buying back ordinary shares in the market.

4. Cash flow can therefore help to indicate:

   1. The trend of liquidity and gearing

   2. If the dividend is safe

   3. If the company has been over-trading

   4. If future capex can be funded from within.

5. A simple additional sieve to apply to low PEG stocks is to ensure that cash flow per share exceeds EPS for the last reported year and for the average of the previous five years.

   This sieve has had little effect either way over the eight six-month periods that have been tested so far. However, the cash flow sieve provides an extra degree of comfort and it is anticipated that it will work better in a bear market.

6. Cash-guzzlers with capex regularly in excess of cash flow per share should be avoided. High owners' earnings is a very desirable criterion for growth shares.

7

RELATIVE STRENGTH

Having substantially narrowed the potential universe of shares with the PEG sieve, and used cash flow to provide some peace of mind, we can now move on to the final stage of the selection process to discover the *real* high flyers. My third sieve is the relative strength of a share price against the market for both the previous month and the previous year. Although it is tempting to think that shares which have underperformed recently have the most potential for growth, in practice the best-performing shares tend to be those that have *already* started behaving like winners by outperforming the market.

I now regard relative strength in the previous twelve months as such an important measure that all of the tables in REFS include a column for it. In addition, we have introduced two special sets of relative strength tables covering each of the indices. I am not alone in believing in the value of relative strength as an investment criterion. In February 1996, *Barrons*, the American weekly investment newspaper, drew attention to a forthcoming book by Jim O'Shaughnessy, who has researched the last 43 years of data from the Standard & Poors CompuStat database. The author tested every conceivable method of investment and found that of the 10 best winning strategies for buying American shares, each of them involved some element of relative strength, judged by the stock's performance relative to other stocks during the previous year.

It is easy to determine if the relative strength of a share price is positive or negative. Say the market, as represented by the FT-SE Actuaries All-Share index, stands at 1800 and the share price of a company is 100p. If the market rises by 18 points during the month, that is 1% of 1800. Unless the company's shares rise by at least 1p, their relative strength would be negative. If the shares rise by 1p, matching the market's growth, their relative strength would be neutral and if the shares rise by more than 1p, their relative strength would be positive.

The way of calculating the *exact* percentage relative strength is a little more complex. Say a share price starts out at 100p and during a given period rises by 10% to 110p while the market increases by 20%. The relative strength of the share during that month would be –8.5%. The market would have risen to 120% of its former level, the shares to 110% of theirs and the 10 percentage points difference between the two represents 8.5% of 120%.

Take another example of a share that fell from 100p to 80p while the market rose by 20%. In this instance, the share would be at 80% of its former level against the market's 120%. The difference of 40 percentage points expressed as a percentage of 120% shows relative strength of –33.3%.

As a final illustration, if the previous example was the other way around, and the share price had risen by 20% to 120p and the market had fallen by 20%, the relative strength would be +50%. The share price would be 120% of its former level, the market 80% and the difference of 40 percentage points would be 50% of 80%. Note that the relative strength percentage is always calculated in relation to the market's performance, which in the first and second instances had risen to 120% of its former value and in the third had fallen to 80%.

The good news is that only the mathematicians among you need worry about how relative strength is worked out. REFS makes all these calculations for subscribers and shows them in the chart in the company entry like the one shown below. As an investor, all you need to

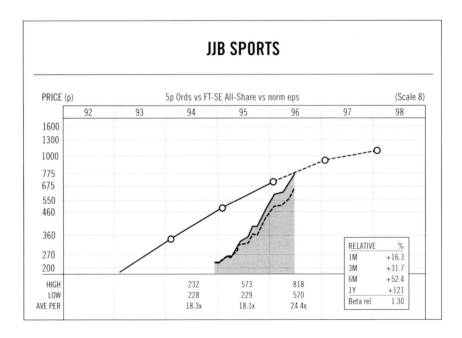

understand is that a share showing positive relative strength is outperforming the rest of the market while one with negative relative strength is faltering.

The relative strength plot is the broken line which usually floats within the shaded area which supports the plot of the share price. The relative strength plot is superimposed and rebased, so that it always starts at the same point as the share price plot.

You will also see the small box to the bottom right of JJB Sports' chart. It shows the relative strength for the previous year, six months, three months and one month. In addition, there are monthly tables of the shares in each index with the lowest and highest relative strength every month and there are columns in the table of shares with the lowest PEGs showing the one-month and one-year relative strength of the shares in question.

THE THIRD SIEVE

There are two requirements for the third sieve of relative strength. First, it should be positive for the previous month (even 0.1% would suffice) *and*, second, for the previous twelve months it should be both positive *and greater* than the one-month figure. The June 1996 charts below show as examples Psion, with excellent relative strength, and Telspec, that is faltering and failed to qualify.

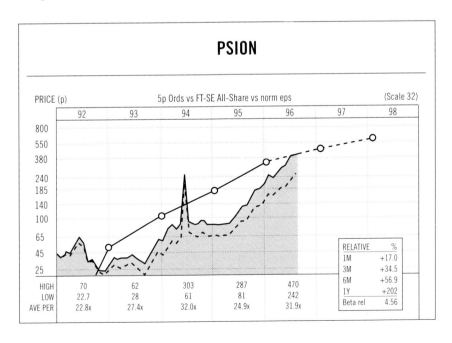

PSION

	PRICE (p)		5p Ords vs FT-SE All-Share vs norm eps			(Scale 32)

	92	93	94	95	96	97	98
HIGH	70	62	303	287	470		
LOW	22.7	28	61	81	242		
AVE PER	22.8x	27.4x	32.0x	24.9x	31.9x		

RELATIVE	%
1M	+17.0
3M	+34.5
6M	+56.9
1Y	+202
Beta rel	4.56

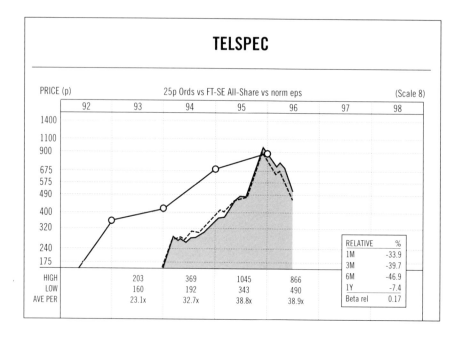

In a bull market, using relative strength as an investment measure works exceptionally well. It identifies companies that are acting like winners. If a share begins to falter in the market, it is quite possible that a number of people know of some bad news that is about to be released and are selling some of their shares.

The very least that an investor should do is to make sure that at the time of purchase the share being bought is acting like a winner and that its future in the stock market *appears* to be set fair.

It is time to look at the results of applying the relative strength sieve to the shares that had already survived the previous PEG and cash flow tests. As you can see from the figures below, the relative strength sieve was a massive success:

| Six months ended | FT-SE All Share Index | Performance of PEGs below 0.6 | |
| | | +cash flow | +cash flow +relative strength |
	%	%	%
30 September 1995	13.0	26.3	45.7
31 October 1995	9.1	20.3	23.4
30 November 1995	9.0	20.4	26.7
31 December 1995	11.0	24.5	45.9
31 January 1996	6.7	18.1	34.1
29 February 1996	5.5	14.9	15.4
31 March 1996	6.4	14.9	39.4
30 April 1996	10.7	33.6	45.7
AVERAGE GAIN	8.9	21.6	34.5

The universe of shares that qualified was reduced from about 25 to an average of only nine, but the results were spectacular. In just six months, the average increase was about 34.5% compared with 21.6% using the cash flow and low PEG sieves and only an 8.9% increase in the market as a whole.

FURTHER PROOF

Further proof of the effectiveness of the sieves of low PEGs, strong cash flow and high relative strength are provided in Chapter 15 on Portfolio Management. I show there the performance of the eight shares selected using all of the sieves for a New Year's portfolio in the *Financial Mail on Sunday.* By the end of June 1996, the eight shares showed an average profit of 22.4% *after all expenses,* and after allowing for the benefit of press comment, while the market as a whole *with no expenses* rose by only 3%.

Yet more proof is provided by my son's fund, The Johnson Fry Slater Growth Unit Trust. Mark began managing this trust in July 1995 and, by 31 October, had switched the portfolio into shares with low PEGs, strong cash flow and high relative strength. By 5 June 1996, the portfolio had appreciated 36.9% *after all costs including management fees* compared with the market's rise of only 11.2%. During that period Slater Growth was also the top performing unit trust in the UK growth sector.

MORE ON RELATIVE STRENGTH

When applying the relative strength sieve for the previous month, it should be borne in mind that after long periods of heady growth, the share prices of great growth stocks sometimes pause for breath. As long as the overall trend is intact, and the company appears to be carrying on doing its thing, this is not necessarily a cause for alarm. For this reason, I sometimes relax my one-month relative strength rule if it is mildly negative, as long as the last three months' relative strength is still positive. However, I have become such a great fan of the twelve months' relative strength rule that I never waver from it.

It is the *continued* weakening of a share price over several months that should cause investors to reconsider the right of a company to a place in their portfolios. The purpose of this chapter is not to examine the courses of action open to them once a share has been bought, but it is abundantly clear that it would be nonsense to *begin* an involvement with a growth company when its shares are starting to act badly against the market. A value investor looking for companies at a discount to assets might disagree, but growth investors should be focused on ensuring that nothing is going wrong with the story of a stock and that the future outlook continues to be rosy.

In a bear market, the relative strength sieve will almost certainly not work so well. The kinds of shares that rise most in a bull market are those that by definition have the best relative strength. In the final stage of a bear market investors rush for cover and, *irrespective of underlying value*, tend to sell those shares that show the most profit. Provided you can last out the storm (fortunately bear markets tend to be relatively brief) the value highlighted by the low PEG and strong cash flow should support the share price and help it to recover. As the market goes up, these kinds of shares are usually the first to recover.

Take a typical low PEG share with a prospective year ahead PER of 15 and a growth rate of 30% per annum. After a year's further growth, if the share price stayed the same, the PER would drop to 11.5. A year after that it would drop to 8.9 and become such an obvious bargain that even the dimmest fund manager would consider buying some.

As an investor who concentrates on the fundamentals, I have always regarded cash flow per share as a more important sieve than relative strength. On the test results so far, however, the relative strength sieve is a hands-down winner over cash flow, so I am more than happy to revise my prejudice.

TECHNICAL ANALYSIS

Chartists work on the assumption that, irrespective of fundamentals like fluctuating multiples and asset values, a chart showing the history of a share price reflects the hopes and fears of all investors. They also argue that prices usually follow a trend and that when they do it is more important to go with it than to try to estimate future profits. Chartists also attempt to establish the best moment to buy a share – a point at which the upside potential is maximised and the downside risk reduced to a minimum.

I have always been sceptical about chartists. However, in recent years I have been converted to believing that charts are an essential tool in an investor's kit and that, in particular, the relative strength of share prices in the previous twelve months is an essential investment sieve.

To clarify my thoughts on chartism, let me itemise my present beliefs about the uses of technical analysis:

1. Charts do provide a quick overall picture of what has happened to a share price over a given period. I particularly like the REFS charts with the share price, relative strength and EPS growth shown in three separate plots. They make it very easy to recognise a good growth share. A steeply rising share price, coupled with high relative strength and a forecast of strong EPS growth beckoning the share price further ahead, is the most encouraging pattern.

2. Chartists and technical analysts use different systems, most of which are based on the well-worn phrase 'the trend is your friend'. Disciples therefore tend to cut their losses and run their profits, which means that they are following the most important of all of the guiding investment principles.

3. A substantial number of investors believe in charts, so some forecasts by chartists become self-fulfilling. A well-known buying signal encourages buying which in turn puts up the price. Conversely, a widely recognised bearish pattern has the reverse effect.

4. The month of the year can be an important factor in deciding when to buy shares. There is no doubt that *historically* some months have been better for investors than others. January is well known as being one of the best months and June as one of the worst. I can see how 'sell in May and go away' became such a well-known stock market maxim.

    There is no doubt that electoral cycles, budgets, the weather and enthusiasm at the beginning of a new year all play their part in making certain months better than others for the stock market. I do, however, part company with those extreme enthusiasts, who would claim, for example, that 19 February is likely to be better or worse than 18 February, just because it has always been a good or bad day in most previous years.

5. The Coppock Indicator is perhaps the single most reliable signal of a bull market. It has not given a false signal since 1948 and the average gain based on the last ten buy signals was 30%. As the Coppock Indicator is calculated on moving averages, it is a relatively easy matter to know when there is a strong likelihood of a bullish signal being given. The Coppock Indicator does not provide reliable sell signals.

6. A break-out, a strong upward movement after a long period of consolidation, often highlights very graphically that something is afoot. Directors' buying or news of a recent management change can provide strong corroborative evidence.

7. A share price breaking through its moving average, while the average itself is improving, is usually a reliable bullish signal. Conversely, a break below the moving average is usually a bearish sign.

SUMMARY

1. Good relative strength in the previous twelve months was a common ingredient of the ten best winning investment strategies examined by Jim O'Shaughnessy when researching the CompuStat database over a 43-year period.

2. In REFS, the relative strength plot is the broken line in the chart of the share price. Detailed figures for one, three and twelve months are also shown in the small box to the bottom right of the chart. There are extensive tables in the tables volume showing the shares with the best and worst relative strength during the previous month and previous year.

3. I recommend as a third sieve positive relative strength over the previous month *and* positive and greater relative strength for the previous twelve months. The results of using these sieves over eight periods of six months lifted the average increase to a spectacular 34.5% compared with 21.6% when only PEGs of under 0.6 and strong cash flow were used as sieves. During the same period the market increased by just 8.9%.

4. Compromises can be made if the one-month relative strength is mildly negative, provided the three-month figure remains positive and all other investment criteria are fully met.

5. The relative strength sieve might not be so effective in a bear market, as investors often panic and take profits irrespective of underlying value.

6. There are a number of other advantages of technical analysis which are set out in detail on pages 70 and 71.

8

—

MANAGEMENT

It is, of course, important to ensure, as far as you are able, that the management of any company in which you invest is both competent and honest. The difficulty arises in judging people from a brief meeting or from reading annual reports, brokers' circulars, magazines and newspapers.

Anybody can see from the wonderful growth record of an established company like Rentokil that its chief executive, Clive Thompson, knows a thing or two about management and is able to inspire his team. Equally, even with a less well-known company like Admiral, it is undoubtedly apparent from the company's ten-year record of unbroken EPS growth that Clay Brendish is doing a first-class job. It is much harder to make a sensible judgement with companies in their very early stages, when the record is insufficient to form a reliable guide to the management's capabilities.

It is important to remember that if the management of a company is intent upon fooling you, all of the cards are stacked in its favour. You might, for example, visit the chief executive of an engineering business with the idea of being shown the factory and then joining a select group of his colleagues afterwards for lunch. You would undoubtedly be impressed if, during your trip around the factory, the chief executive explained in detail the inner workings of a new state-of-the-art machine that was about to transform the profitability of the company's core business. You would also be impressed if he put his arm around the shoulders of one of the operatives and said, 'Fred's been with us eighteen years now – how's the new baby, Fred?' From these two incidents you would probably gain the impression that the chief executive had a good personal relationship with the work force and, into the bargain, was technically gifted.

It is, of course, possible that you would be right. However, there is also a chance that the chief executive had studied the technical details of just one or two machines and that his relationship with Fred was part of his act when showing visitors around the factory. It is even possible that Fred's name was really Charlie, but he was too frightened to say so.

In the same vein, you can imagine how, over lunch with the other executives, the conversation could be kept away from problems with a new product or the impending strike at one of their factories. Instead, it could easily be steered towards a pleasing increase in like-for-like sales and the overhead savings and other benefits arising from a recent acquisition.

The point to bear in mind is that you would be meeting the chief executive in an environment which he knows and controls, so you would be seeing him at his very best. It is a very different matter if a relationship is developed with management that has been tried and tested over a long period. On many occasions, I have met chief executives who impressed me and my investments in their companies turned out to be exceptionally profitable. Over a period of a few years, I have got to know the managements in question and my confidence in them gradually increased as they continued to deliver on their promises to shareholders. I regret to say there is an equally long list of managers who have been very disappointing.

Perhaps the most useful aspect of a visit to a company is the opportunity to observe the general behaviour and attitude of the executives and staff. Is the telephone answered quickly, pleasantly and efficiently? Is the receptionist alert and on-the-ball? Do the staff deal with enquiries promptly and seem to have a sense of purpose? Are the personnel you speak to *enthusiastic* about the company and obviously proud of it? Are they the kind of people you would like to employ? In a word, is there a corporate spirit that will make your investment a winner?

WAYS OF CHECKING MANAGEMENT

Here are some further suggestions for improving your appreciation of the management of any company in which you invest and for monitoring it to make sure that it does not go astray:

1. *Annual general meetings*

    It is a good idea to attend AGMs to see whether or not they are well organised and how well the chairman and the chief executive field questions. Bear in mind though that, even at AGMs, management often arranges for a few prepared questions to be raised.

2. *Annual reports*

Overly lavish annual reports littered with colour photographs, especially of the chairman and other directors, are usually a worrying sign. The best-known example was Spring Ram, which took the opportunity each year to stress an annual theme such as 'Winning Through Teamwork'. After a major setback it was not long before the founder, Bill Rooney, was removed from that team in response to institutional pressure.

The auditor's report should, of course, be checked to ensure that there is no qualification of any kind. You should also always read the detailed notes to the report and accounts, as sometimes very significant points are tucked away in the small print.

3. *Constitution of boards*

Many years ago, there were a few amusing articles in one of the Sunday papers suggesting a points system for assessing the quality of the board of directors. I cannot remember exactly how plus points were gained, but I do remember that deductions were made for politicians, admirals and the like. I suppose the underlying thought was that politicians and admirals might be on the board simply for the sake of appearances, as opposed to any contribution they were likely to make to a company's progress.

4. *The chief executive's outside activities*

Beware of chief executives who are always sounding off about their industry and always seem to be giving interviews about the state of the country and industry in general. They might be thinking too much about the possibility of being knighted and too little about the company that employs them.

5. *Lifestyle of the company's key executives*

Beware of companies with chief executives who live in an overtly flashy way with personalised number plates, aeroplanes, houses owned by the company and the like.

It can be a bad sign if the chief executive acquires a substantial financial interest in a football club or becomes chairman of one.

6. *Failure to meet profit forecasts*

Any chief executive who fails to meet a formal profit forecast is on a slippery slope. Institutional backing will be much harder to obtain next time around, so further fund-raising capacity might be put in jeopardy. Even failing by a wide margin to live up to the brokers' consensus forecast can be a serious problem. If the analytical skills of a large number of highly paid brokers are put in doubt, they will want to blame someone.

7. *Calibre of advisers*

As the future progress of many growing companies depends to a large extent upon share placings, the calibre of the company's stockbrokers, merchant bankers and investing institutions is a material consideration. A first-class incoming executive team will invariably attract top-level support.

With all my investments, I concentrate mainly on the financial statistics. However, I keep an eye on pointers like these to give me the feel of a company and of the chief executive running it. In my sometimes bitter experience, these kinds of measures can often give you a better general impression than you would obtain by making a company visit or meeting the chief executive for lunch.

CHIEF EXECUTIVE OFFICER CHANGES

The appointment of a new chief executive can herald the complete transformation of a company. This is especially the case if the incoming CEO is someone of high repute with a good track record and the company he is joining is known to be poorly managed.

The appointment of Archie Norman as CEO of Asda and Gerry Robinson as CEO of Granada were obvious examples. The two charts below begin when the appointments were made and show that they were followed by very substantial advances in the companies' share prices.

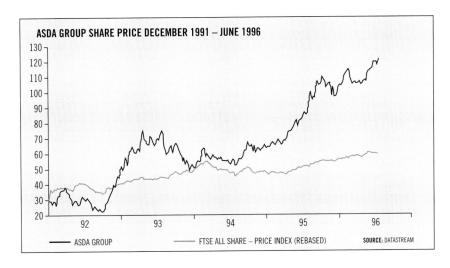

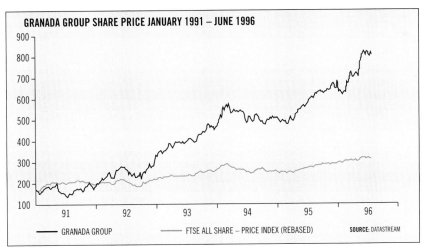

It is often difficult to determine if a new CEO is really capable. It is always worth trying to check the EPS growth record of the CEO's previous company, but often insufficient information is available, so investors have to rely upon newspaper comment and profiles in magazines.

REFS gives details of changes of CEOs during the previous twelve months, together with the actual words used in the press releases. Formal announcements of the retirement of CEOs have to be read with a pinch of salt. Sometimes they are completely genuine, but on other occasions 'Retirement due to ill-health' can mean 'Judged incompetent by common acclaim' and 'Wishes to reduce his executive responsibilities' is a polite way of saying 'He has done enough damage to the company already.'

It should be borne in mind that the other side of the coin to a very capable new CEO being appointed is that he or she can be tempted away by a better offer. It is therefore unwise to place too much reliance on the new CEO and to concentrate on ensuring that the underlying business is sound. Managers are mobile and frequently hop from one company to another, as George Simpson's move from Lucas to GEC demonstrates only too well.

A superb new CEO is a major reason for investing in a company, but it should not be the only reason. Warren Buffett's wry observation bears this out: 'When a management with a reputation for brilliance tackles a business with a reputation for poor fundamental economics, it is the reputation of the business that remains intact.'

DIRECTORS' SHARE DEALINGS

It is undoubtedly encouraging to know that the directors of a company own a large number of shares, so that their money is where their mouth is, alongside your investment.

Before finally selecting a share to buy or sell, investors should, as a matter of routine, always make themselves aware of recent share dealings by directors. It is pertinent to note that in an August 1993 study, Smith New Court (now part of Merrill Lynch) demonstrated that simply by following directors' dealings an investor could have outperformed the stock market.

The most important thing to bear in mind is that directors' buying is far more important than directors' selling. A director investing a significant amount of cash in his or her company presumably feels that the shares are undervalued and are a better investment than cash. The same argument does not necessarily apply in reverse. The director may have decided that the shares are overvalued, but equally the money could be needed for another perfectly valid purpose – to buy a new house, meet a call from Lloyds or simply fund an expensive lifestyle.

Another important point is the number of directors buying or selling. If a cluster of them buys shares, this substantially strengthens the buying signal. The selling signal is also much clearer if a number of directors are unloading shares.

The significance of the share deals in relation to the number of shares a director holds is also highly relevant. So is the position of the director who is dealing. A purchase of 10,000 shares by a chairman who already owns over one million shares is of no particular importance – he might just be showing the flag at a time of difficulty. But a finance director doubling his holding from 10,000 to 20,000 is a strong message. Similarly, a sales director selling 10,000 shares out of a holding of only 12,000 would put me on red alert.

BLACKS LEISURE GROUP – Retailers, general					
31.8m 50p Ords:					*Holding*
T W Knight	Nov-6	P	+50,000 @ 50.0p	£25,000	171,396
S A Bentley (ch & ce)	Jan-5	P	+50,000 @ 64.0p	£32,000	285,500
T W Knight	Jan-5	P	+50,000 @ 64.0p	£32,000	221,396
P D Bennett	Jan-5	P	+5,000 @ 64.0p	£3,200	10,000
Sir Rhodes Boyson*	Jan-5	P	+10,000 @ 64.0p	£6,400	40,000
D A Bernstein*	Jan-5	P	+50,000 @ 64.0p	£32,000	50,000
S A Bentley (ch & ce)	Feb-29	P	+25,000 @ 69.0p	£17,250	310,500
T W Knight	Feb-29	P	+40,000 @ 69.0p	£27,600	261,396
D A Bernstein*	Feb-29	P	+50,000 @ 69.0p	£34,500	100,000

The above schedule of directors' dealings is taken from the tables volume of the April 1996 issue of REFS. As you can see it is a classic example of a cluster of directors buying a significant number of shares in relation to their existing holdings. I was attracted to the shares by the first tranche of buying at 64p in January 1996 and bought some after the February tranche at 69p. In late May, the company's annual results showed a massive increase in profits and the company's broker forecast further very substantial progress in the current year. The day after the announcement the shares rose to 160p.

A director buying shares on appointment is no great cause for joy, unless the purchase is a very substantial one. Also, buying shares to take up an option that is expiring is not as significant as buying in the normal way. However, if the extra shares from the option are retained, this can be encouraging.

Companies have 'close periods' before their results when directors cannot deal in the shares. It is useful to know the key dates, as, in retrospect, dealings about a month before close periods begin often appear to be very astute.

The easiest way to find details of directors' dealings is to ask your broker. His screens show dealings on a daily basis and he should be able to provide details of the preceding few months' transactions.

REFS shows the last six months of directors' dealings in great detail together with a mass of other statistical information, including the director's position, the nature of the transaction and the residual shareholding. Although dealings by several directors can be an interesting investment pointer, they are no substitute for a detailed examination of the company's financial figures and prospects. However, when you have made a decision to buy, it is always pleasing to find that the directors agree with you and are also buying shares. Conversely, when you see that they have been unloading in a big way, it is difficult to muster much enthusiasm for a company.

SUMMARY

1. With mature companies, the record of EPS growth is one of the best ways to judge the capability of management.

2. With less mature companies, the EPS growth rate is of great importance, but the record may not be long enough to judge the management's ability.

3. If managers are intent upon fooling investors, the cards are stacked in their favour. Investors should try to build a picture from:

   a) Annual general meetings

   b) Annual reports

   c) Constitution of the board

d) The CEO's outside activities and lifestyle

e) Success or failure in meeting profit forecasts

f) Calibre of advisers

Additionally, the attitude of employees can be a good guide. Is the phone answered quickly, do they have a sense of purpose and are they proud of their company?

4. The appointment of a new CEO can herald a major change in a company's fortunes. Read press cuttings and profiles and try to ascertain the incoming CEO's record of increasing EPS in his previous employment.

5. Directors' share dealings are a useful guide to share selection. In particular, a cluster of directors buying is a very bullish sign.

The position of the director and the percentage increase or decrease in residual shareholding should also be taken into account. Note that dealings just before the close period often appear to be very astute in retrospect.

6. REFS gives comprehensive details every month of CEO changes during the preceding twelve months and directors' dealings during the preceding six months.

9

—

COMPETITIVE ADVANTAGE

The competitive advantage of a company underpins future earnings and increases the reliability of profit forecasts. Sometimes called 'a business franchise', it can arise in several different ways:

1.   *Top-class brand names*

Coca-Cola, McDonalds, Marks & Spencer (St Michael) and Sony spring to mind.

2.   *Patents or copyrights*

Glaxo Wellcome's Zantac was, for many years, an excellent example. Copyrights for records, books and films now have immense value with growing worldwide demand from cable and satellite television.

3.   *Legal monopolies*

Water and electricity companies are protected from competition, but they are also regulated. Companies in television, like Carlton and Granada, have immensely valuable franchises, although they are subject to renewal in the longer term.

4.   *Dominance in an industry*

Businesses like the *Wall Street Journal* and the *Financial Times*, Microsoft, Disney and Rentokil are leading examples.

5.   *An established position in a niche market*

Druck Holdings is a prime example of a high-quality UK company specialising in a niche market – the manufacture and sale of electronic pressure, force measuring and temperature calibration devices. As the chart shows, Druck has been a wonderful growth share.

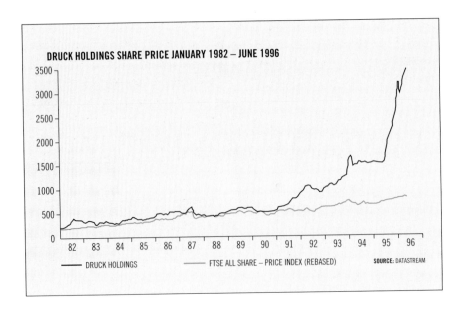

DRUCK HOLDINGS SHARE PRICE JANUARY 1982 – JUNE 1996

DRUCK HOLDINGS   FTSE ALL SHARE – PRICE INDEX (REBASED)   SOURCE: DATASTREAM

Given the choice, it is obviously better to invest in businesses that have a distinct advantage over their competitors, making them less vulnerable to attack. Businesses like Reuters and Marks & Spencer have strong business franchises that make them difficult to compete with. In contrast, businesses which do not have a franchise of any kind, like small restaurants, builders and decorators and general engineering businesses, are very unattractive to investors. There are no barriers to entry, so almost anyone can set up in opposition to them with only a small capital outlay and very little difficulty. Their failure rate is therefore high, as margins frequently come under pressure.

Warren Buffett invests almost exclusively in businesses with very strong business franchises – companies like Coca-Cola, American Express and Disney. He sums up this important facet of his investment philosophy in his own inimitable manner:

The test of a franchise is what a smart guy with a lot of money could do to it if he tried. If you gave me a billion dollars, and you gave me first draft pick of fifty business managers throughout the United States, I could cream both the business world and the journalistic world. If you said, 'Go take the *Wall Street Journal*', I would hand you back the billion dollars.

Now, incidentally, if you gave me a similar amount of money and you told me to make a dent in the profitability of or change the market position of the Omaha National Bank or the leading department store in Omaha, I could give them a very hard time. I might not do much for you in the process, but I would cause them a lot of trouble. The real test of a business is how much damage a competitor can do, even if he is stupid about returns.

There are some businesses that have very large moats around them with crocodiles, sharks and piranhas in. Those are the sorts of businesses you want. You want some business that, going back to my day, Johnny Weissmuller in a suit of armour could not make it across the moat. There are businesses like that.

THE RIGHT SECTOR

As I explained in Chapter 3, some business sectors are much more attractive than others. Media, Pharmaceuticals and Support Services, for example, have a tail wind behind them. In contrast, shipbuilding, heavy engineering and textiles are constantly fighting against a head wind – they are all highly labour intensive and are bound to suffer increasingly from international competition from cheap labour countries.

The importance of making sure that you do not invest in the wrong sector was emphasised by Richard Branson when he was asked how to become a millionaire. 'That's easy,' he replied. 'First, you become a billionaire and then you buy an airline.'

The monthly tables volume of REFS contains full details of each sector. For example, the table below, taken from the May 1996 issue, shows the Breweries, Pubs and Restaurants sector.

The constituents of the sector are listed in order of market capitalisation. The table shows each company's exact position, how its key statistics, particularly its ROCE, profit margin and price-to-sales ratio, compare with the average of both the market and the sector and with the other members of its peer group.

The tables are obviously useful once a potential candidate for investment has been identified. They are even more useful for spotting new candidates in favoured sectors.

BREWERIES, PUBS & RESTAURANTS

Mkt Cap £m	Rel str 1 Mo %	Rel str 1 Yr %	Recent Share Price (p)	Company	Prosp PER	5-Year Eps Growth Rate %	Prosp Eps Growth Rate %	Prosp PEG	Prosp DY %	Last AR PSR	Last AR Profit Margin %
8,979	−0.0	−0.6	569	Market weighted average	14.2	10.6	13.1	1.6	4.2	4.4	12.7
46.7	+0.0	−2.7	138	Market median	13.1	4.8	14.0	1.1	3.8	0.9	7.8
3,828	+2.9	+15.5	682	Sector weighted average	16.5	3.1	11.9	1.5	3.5	1.7	13.8
58.4	+0.8	+11.6	285	Sector median	16.0	8.5	12.3	1.3	2.8	1.7	13.6
6,897	+0.8	+17.6	782	Bass	15.6	−3.0	9.5	1.6	4.1	1.5	14.4
4,230	+4.1	+8.0	691	Scottish & Newcastle	15.3	4.2	16.5	0.9	3.8	1.8	15.2
3,625	+6.4	+9.4	750	Whitbread	16.0	−2.4	9.8	1.6	3.9	1.5	8.3
1,840	+4.1	+13.0	625	Greenalls	15.5	1.2	10.9	1.4	3.2	1.7	17.6
1,723	+0.3	+36.0	549	Compass Group	19.4	12.1	15.5	1.2	2.1	0.9	6.1
446	−0.1	+5.7	667	Wolverhampton & Dudley	14.6	2.6	5.5	2.7	3.3	1.9	18.4
436	+10.3	+9.0	310	Vaux	15.4	−6.2	7.8	2.0	4.4	1.7	18.4
341	−2.1	+49.1	888	Wetherspoon (JD)	24.7	37.5	24.2	1.0	1.5	4.7	17.7
313	−1.9	−0.3	349	Marston, Thompson	14.8	9.0	5.8	2.5	2.8	2.0	17.2
295	+6.1	+11.5	695	Greene King	15.3	2.1	7.6	2.0	3.0	1.9	18.4
233	+25.5	+21.9	121	City Centre Restaurants	24.2	5.8	9.9	na	2.1	2.2	11.6
223	+5.0	+15.8	345	Mansfield Brewery	15.3	14.7	9.7	1.6	2.4	1.7	13.6
202	+6.2	+112	349	PizzaExpress	28.3	88.3	20.7	1.4	1.0	6.1	20.2
184	−2.4	+23.7	670	Morland	16.4	12.8	9.3	1.8	2.5	2.4	21.4
163	−5.0	+127	£10.1	Regent Inns	20.9	38.6	29.7	0.7	1.5	6.8	23.0
158	+2.6	+53.0	402	Yates Bros Wine Lodges	25.1	na	24.0	1.0	1.3	2.8	9.8
103	+8.7	+62.9	142	Pelican Group	16.9	25.3	16.7	1.0	2.1	3.0	12.6
102	−3.6	−18.0	£33.5	Holt (Joseph)	16.7	13.0	9.1	na	2.4	3.6	24.4
99.7	−1.3	+11.6	489	Fuller Smith & Turner	15.3	0.6	12.3	1.2	2.6	1.4	11.2
97.7	+0.7	+94.9	354	Ascot Hldgs	41.2	6.8	−40.3	na	na	0.8	26.2
87.7	+2.5	na	220	Cobleigh (Tom)	21.6	na	14.6	1.5	1.8	3.3	17.7
70.4	+9.0	na	174	Enterprise Inns	10.4	na	31.4	0.3	5.2	2.9	41.8
62.4	−6.6	+4.3	312	Hardys & Hansons	13.9	4.6	3.6	3.9	4.5	1.8	21.1
54.5	+1.1	+42.2	260	Eldridge Pope	15.5	55.1	12.2	1.3	2.6	1.0	9.3
52.6	+1.8	na	133	Century Inns	8.5	na	−3.8	na	6.7	1.2	40.4
44.9	−4.1	−34.8	323	Gibbs Mew	9.4	14.0	13.2	0.7	4.2	0.9	13.8
43.4	−2.4	+3.8	490	Young & Co's Brewery	21.8	−1.9	−12.6	na	3.8	0.9	9.7
42.0	+4.8	+65.9	225	Groupe Chez Gerard	17.3	na	23.8	0.7	1.9	3.2	15.8
36.5	+5.9	+14.1	145	My Kinda Town	13.5	na	16.5	na	3.1	1.3	12.9
34.6	−5.8	−11.5	166	Burtonwood Brewery	13.6	−11.9	7.0	na	4.5	0.7	8.8
34.0	+0.2	+18.7	240	Grosvenor Inns	16.0	na	27.6	0.6	3.5	2.2	13.0
28.8	−3.8	+0.8	326	Ramsden's (Harry)	38.4	10.7	9.0	na	1.9	6.6	28.3
25.7	+13.2	−10.2	54	Inn Business	22.7	64.1	na	na	na	0.8	12.6
23.2	+1.9	na	315	Jennings Brothers (AIM)	22.4	8.0	0.2	na	2.5	1.6	10.8
22.2	+15.7	na	210	Surrey Free Inns (AIM)	24.2	38.3	104	na	1.1	1.8	13.1
13.5	−3.6	na	110	Old English Pub Co (AIM)	86.6	na	na	na	na	3.7	11.8
12.5	−6.1	+1.9	185	Heavitree Brewery	11.3	20.5	16.1	na	3.9	1.4	21.2
11.7	+3.5	na	73	Ask Central (AIM)	42.7	na	na	na	na	11.5	−0.9
10.9	−5.6	−11.6	46	Break for the Border	10.0	na	58.6	PEG	4.9	0.4	8.9
5.40	−3.6	na	18	Greenhills (AIM)	na	na	na	na	na	na	na
5.31	−24.5	−53.5	4.5	Paramount	6.5	−17.8	16.2	na	7.9	0.8	20.5
5.28	+2.1	na	18	Celebrated Grp (AIM)	24.7	na	82.5	na	na	1.3	12.1
5.20	+40.7	na	178	Cafe Inns (AIM)	15.1	3.2	75.5	na	1.4	0.4	10.5
4.56	−3.6	+25.5	38	Aberdeen Steak Houses	12.7	60.9	−11.0	na	na	0.3	4.8
2.51	−3.6	−17.0	9.5	Courtyard Leisure	−12.5	−25.5	na	na	na	1.1	−6.8
1.68	−0.7	na	35	Dalkeith (AIM)	41.7	29.8	na	na	na	0.5	2.1

THE KEY STATISTICS

Another important investment aid in the companies volume is the key statistics panel for each company, which I touched on in Chapter 4. The top five statistics – the PER, PEG, growth rate, ROCE and margin – are grouped together as they are all key figures for growth investors. The bottom five are of more interest to value investors and the dividend yield and gearing are of equal interest to both.

The moons headed M and S show, at a glance, how each company's statistics compare with the market and its sector average, giving a quick and clear indication of whether a company is made of the right stuff for growth or value investors. The blacker the moons the better, so a cluster of solid black moons indicates that a company is well worth further investigation.

The moons are calibrated to show the exact position of a company in its sector and in the market as a whole. For example, in a sector containing nine companies, if the company under review was in fifth position the sector moon would be half full.

JJB SPORTS				
PRICE (NMS 1) 27-NOV-95				**510p**
norm eps (pr)				33.4p
market cap				£153m
turnover (95AR)				£61.3m
pretax (95AR)				£7.59m
			m	s
DY (pr)	%	2.71		
PER (pr)	x	15.3		
PEG (pr)	f	0.32	●	●
GR (pr)	%	48.2	●	●
ROCE	%	34.8	●	●
MARGIN	%	12.4		●
GEAR	%	−53.3	●	●
PBV	x	7.09		
PTBV	x	7.09		
PCF	x	23.8		
PSR	x	2.17		
PRR	x	na		
non-index company				
market overall				496th

HARTSTONE GROUP				
PRICE (NMS 25) 27-NOV-95				**14.5p**
norm eps (pr)				1.77p
market cap				£47.0m
turnover (95AR)				£218m
pretax (95AR)				£4.70m
			m	s
DY (pr)	%	3.97		
PER (pr)	x	8.20	●	●
PEG	f	na		
GR (pr)	%	12.8		
ROCE	%	9.31		
MARGIN	%	4.39		
GEAR	%	57.6		
PBV	x	0.88	●	●
PTBV	x	0.88	●	●
PCF	x	3.35	●	●
PSR	x	0.17	●	●
PRR	x	na		
FT-SE SmallCap				472nd
market overall				931st

PRESSAC HOLDINGS				
PRICE (NMS 2) 27-NOV-95				**142p**
norm eps (pr)				11.2p
market cap				£52.7m
turnover (95AR)				£57.3m
pretax (95AR)				£4.61m
			m	s
DY (pr)	%	3.51		
PER (pr)	x	12.7		●
PEG (pr)	f	0.75		●
GR (pr)	%	17.0		●
ROCE	%	16.2		●
MARGIN	%	8.62		●
GEAR	%	15.9		
PBV	x	2.24		●
PTBV	x	2.34		●
PCF	x	6.97		●
PSR	x	0.82		●
PRR	x	55.7		
FT-SE Fledgling				34th
market overall				893rd

Set out above are the key statistics for JJB Sports, The Hartstone Group and Pressac Holdings, taken from the December 1995 issue of REFS. As can readily be seen, JJB Sports appeared to be a classic growth company with very black moons for all the growth statistics, except the PER, which was about average. The Hartstone Group had little to commend its growth prospects, but was more of an asset situation with solid black moons against all of the relevant value statistics. Pressac Holdings combined some quite strong growth statistics with some reasonably attractive value statistics. It was a kind of hybrid – a growth share that passed through several value filters.

In the case of JJB Sports it was reassuring for growth investors to note that its ROCE and margin showed up well with very black moons. Many growth companies, like Rentokil, Reuters, Next, Medeva, Halma and Druck, shared this very important characteristic in December 1995.

RENTOKIL GROUP

			m	s
DY (pr)	%	1.90		
PER (pr)	x	19.2		
PEG (pr)	f	0.97		
GR (pr)	%	19.8		
ROCE	%	78.1	●	●
MARGIN	%	24.0	●	●
GEAR	%	−38.4	●	●

REUTERS

			m	s
DY (pr)	%	2.19		
PER (pr)	x	22.4		
PEG (pr)	f	1.68		
GR (pr)	%	13.3		
ROCE	%	63.5	●	●
MARGIN	%	20.0	●	●
GEAR	%	−2.94	●	●

NEXT

			m	s
DY (pr)	%	3.62		
PER (pr)	x	17.9		
PEG (pr)	f	1.63		
GR (pr)	%	11.0		
ROCE	%	33.6	●	●
MARGIN	%	13.8	●	●
GEAR	%	−41.0	●	●

HALMA

			m	s
DY (pr)	%	2.10		
PER (pr)	x	18.0		
PEG (pr)	f	1.15		
GR (pr)	%	15.6		
ROCE	%	41.9	●	●
MARGIN	%	18.8	●	●
GEAR	%	−19.8	●	●

DRUCK HOLDINGS

			m	s
DY (pr)	%	0.90		
PER (pr)	x	23.5		
PEG (pr)	f	1.40		
GR (pr)	%	16.9		
ROCE	%	26.1	●	●
MARGIN	%	18.8	●	●
GEAR	%	−5.39	●	●

MEDEVA

			m	s
DY (pr)	%	2.11		●
PER (pr)	x	14.1		●
PEG (pr)	f	0.86		●
GR (pr)	%	16.4		●
ROCE	%	82.1	●	●
MARGIN	%	26.6	●	●
GEAR	%	−7.26	●	●

It is sometimes hard to ascertain a company's competitive advantage simply by general enquiry. However, the strength and trend of a company's ROCE and margin can highlight the edge it has over its competitors.

RETURN ON CAPITAL EMPLOYED

The ROCE measures the return a company achieves on all the capital it employs. To calculate ROCE you simply take the pre-tax profit, before all borrowing costs, and express it as a percentage of the capital the company has employed in its business.

Capital employed in the business is the sum of all ordinary and preference share capital, reserves, all classes of debt and finance lease obligations, minority interests and provisions. The aim is for the final figure to indicate how much capital (whatever the source) is being employed in the operation of the business.

To calculate the return on capital, take the profit before tax, exceptional items, interest and dividends payable. The percentage that this return bears to the capital employed provides an indication of the efficiency the company achieves in working its business assets.

In addition to the strength and trend of ROCE, other factors to be considered when reviewing it include:

1. The ROCE of a company should always be compared with the current cost of borrowing. If the ROCE is significantly higher, further borrowing adds to EPS; if the ROCE is lower, further borrowing will reduce EPS. A good ROCE is therefore essential to a business's ability to raise capital and use it to expand.

2. Companies with low ROCE are often the subject of changes in management control which, in turn, are frequently followed by a rights issue. The acid test of new management is whether or not it is able to lift the return on capital employed.

3. The obvious attraction of a good ROCE is that a higher than average proportion of profits can be ploughed back into the business for the advantage of shareholders. The plough-back is then employed again at the higher than average rate and helps to generate further growth in EPS. For this reason, a high ROCE is usually a common denominator of great growth stocks.

EXCLUSION OF INTANGIBLES

A significant concern when calculating ROCE is the treatment of intangible assets, notably goodwill, but also brands, patents, copyrights, newspaper titles and the like. Such assets can be of immense value, but under UK Generally Accepted Accounting Principles (GAAP), the accounting treatment can vary considerably. For example, in one company brand names will have no value, probably because they have been generated from within. In another comparable company, the value of brands, because they have been acquired, can be a major element of the net assets operating in the business and this will be reflected in the balance sheet.

Only by excluding all intangible assets can a comparable benchmark be achieved. This will indicate the efficiency of the company's operations in working the capital it employs to run its business. However, no two businesses are the same and some are intrinsically more capital intensive than others. At one extreme, in heavy engineering, there is likely to be substantial capital employed in plant and machinery. In a subscription publishing operation, by contrast, with all income received in advance, there could even be a negative value for capital employed.

The most common form of intangible asset is goodwill. Yet this is essentially the mathematical difference between the price paid for the business and the book value of the net assets acquired. It is not an 'asset' employed in the acquired business. It is a fixed sum and as a consequence, and unlike equipment and working capital, is not an asset capable of being managed economically on an ongoing basis. In REFs, therefore, the ROCE statistics measure the return on acquired companies against their underlying operating assets, not against the purchase considerations paid by the acquiring companies.

By excluding intangibles from the calculation of ROCE, REFS provides:

1. A consistent basis for analysis and treatment across all companies.

2. A key measurement of the operating efficiency of the company's working assets.

3. A reflection of the efficiency of working assets acquired through a takeover, but not necessarily an indication that the acquirer paid the right price.

Most investors need not concern themselves with the methodology of calculating ROCE as their brokers should be able to supply the details. REFS gives the ROCE of each company every month and has tables of those companies showing, index by index, the highest returns on capital employed. Because the REFS calculations exclude intangibles, acquisitive companies, that have purchased highly profitable businesses employing little or no capital, may show some extremely high returns – EMAP is an excellent example.

A high ROCE, in the region of 20% or more, is validation of the company's competitive advantage. It indicates the company has something special to offer – products or services that command a high return, which will usually be reflected in above-average margins.

FT-SE 100 – HIGHEST RETURNS ON CAPITAL EMPLOYED

Highest percentage returns on capital employed (excluding intangibles)

Mkt Cap £m	Rel str 1 Mo %	Rel str 1 Yr %	Share price (p) 12 Months High	12 Months Low	Recent	Company	Last AR ROCE	ROCE Trend %pa	Prosp PER	Prosp Eps Growth Rate %	5-Year Eps Growth Rate %	Last AR Margin %
12,858	−0.8	−1.6			640	Index weighted average	30.0	+13.3	14.4	9.4	11.1	16.5
3,892	−0.1	+0.1			525	Index median	18.8	+4.2	14.3	10.1	7.1	13.3
8,112	+4.4	+58.5	480	267	473	British Sky Broadcasting ...	415	+636	27.5	33.4	na	31.5
6,485	−0.3	+18.2	£12.1	855	£11.5	Reed International	77.8	−0.9	22.1	na	13.4	21.1
3,725	+0.6	+20.8	386	263	378	Rentokil	66.3	+17.7	21.1	18.2	23.6	24.4
12,778	+3.2	+33.0	794	479	761	Reuters	56.7	+12.3	25.0	13.3	16.4	20.4
19,071	+4.1	+19.1	726	501	696	SmithKline Beecham	54.7	+11.0	17.9	8.4	11.7	21.4
27,777	−6.9	−10.9	969	721	793	Glaxo Wellcome	43.2	−8.5	13.6	12.7	12.5	34.3
5,090	−1.4	−5.5	561	459	512	Cadbury Schweppes	43.1	+16.4	14.3	1.9	8.3	13.6
3,058	+4.3	−7.2	723	621	720	Reckitt & Colman	41.0	+13.4	13.9	15.0	2.3	14.6
2,139	−1.3	+20.6	720	506	708	Smiths Industries	40.2	−4.9	18.1	13.4	3.3	15.7
7,948	+5.7	+34.0	£18.6	£12.4	£18.5	THORN EMI	39.9	+10.0	22.5	12.5	0.3	9.9
8,008	+4.2	−11.3	280	201	262	Vodafone	39.6	+13.5	22.4	20.6	12.6	31.3
2,703	−1.2	+1.5	484	373	464	Carlton Comms	37.7	+12.3	15.5	11.2	11.5	15.7
6,985	+6.0	+19.5	842	594	824	Granada	34.0	+20.5	17.5	16.7	23.0	15.7
2,065	−1.0	−9.2	203	168	188	Smith & Nephew	33.9	+12.0	15.4	7.4	4.5	18.0
1,914	−11.3	+27.4	683	427	628	Argos	31.5	−1.3	19.0	15.0	14.1	7.7
3,535	+4.7	−8.4	401	310	375	Scottish Power	29.1	+22.6	9.6	14.6	na	22.1
13,197	−1.1	+27.4	£14.1	948	£13.9	Zeneca	28.3	+13.8	19.2	12.4	8.4	18.3
3,391	−1.5	na	211	190	199	National Grid Group	27.7	+15.6	7.9	1.6	na	47.5
2,031	+7.2	−13.2	355	304	350	Williams Holdings	27.0	+2.7	14.2	8.1	1.5	15.2
3,242	+4.1	−3.6	293	220	273	Tomkins	26.9	+26.0	13.1	10.1	7.5	7.7

In the May 1996 issue of REFS, great growth companies such as Reuters and Rentokil were very near the top of the FT-SE 100 ROCE table. As you can see, most of the companies had a trend of ROCE that was improving and in almost every case margins were also at very healthy levels.

RETURN ON INVESTMENT

An alternative way of viewing a company's performance is to consider the Return On Investment (ROI). REFS has just begun to look into the practicality of calculating this further growth statistic. ROI enables investors to tell how the rate of return compares with the cost of invested capital and whether or not the companies in question are creating value for investors or destroying it.

The ROI will be a guide to valuing the company as a whole, including the value that the market has itself placed on the company's acquisition policies and abilities. A company with a high ROI is worth a substantial premium over a company with a poor one. The success of an acquisitive company in making successful deals does not necessarily imply that it can successfully manage them to obtain premium returns on the assets involved in the business. Equally, a company that has a superior record of achieving a high ROCE may not be able to complete successfully acquisitions at value-enhancing prices. This may be due to its inability to integrate fully the new acquisitions with its existing businesses or because it has been pressed into paying too high a premium for its acquisitions.

Like any other investment measure, the ROI should not be looked at in isolation and is best regarded as yet another arrow in the investor's quiver.

OPERATING MARGIN

The second indicator of a strong competitive advantage is the kind of margin that a company can obtain on its products or services. Put very simply, margin is the ratio of operating profit to turnover. For example, a company with operating profits (trading profit before tax, interest and contribution from associated companies) of £10m and a turnover of £100m would have an operating margin of 10%.

Margin is an important investment measure, but there are a number of caveats to be borne in mind:

1. Very high margins invite competition. Unless the barriers to entry are very strong, other companies will be attracted to the industry. Ideally a company will combine high margins with products or services that are 'unique' and difficult to emulate; well-patented products are a good example.

2. Very low margins obviously add to the risk of any investment. A small fall in sales can have a disproportionate and sometimes disastrous effect on profits. Equally, the slightest upward movement can be very beneficial.

3. Major changes in margins frequently occur as a result of new top management. The recent record of margins should therefore be looked at with this in mind.

    Seek an explanation if a company has had the same management for years and margins appear to be changing substantially. A downward spiral could be due, for example, to a price war; an improvement might be the result of new and improved products.

4. Bear in mind that companies with a history of low margins, in industries that have become used to them, find it difficult to increase their margins. In these kinds of businesses, treat with scepticism extravagant claims by new managements about future increases in margins.

5. Any significant improvement of margins is usually based upon some kind of product or service enhancement. Try to identify these from press cuttings or brokers' circulars. Whenever you have the opportunity, ask managers for a detailed explanation of their policy and their long-term goals for margins.

6. Very choppy margin records usually indicate businesses in industries which are subject to periodic price wars and/or are very cyclical. Beware of buying into such companies during a period of very high margins, unless there is strong evidence that there has been a fundamental change and it really will be different this time around.

   The level of sales should always be considered in relation to margins. Rapidly increasing sales can often be at their expense. However, if sales can be increased and margins maintained or expanded, this will naturally result in substantially increased profits.

7. *The profit margins of a company should be compared with the margins of other companies in its peer group and with the sector average.* They sometimes differ considerably for obvious reasons. As you can see from the key statistics on page 88, Druck Holdings' and Halma's margins were identical at 18.8% and, as the black moons indicated, they were both near the top of their sector. At that time other well-known engineering companies, like IMI (7.9%), Weir Group (6.8%), APV (2.3%) and Renold (8.9%), were not faring so well.

8. Once the level of margins has been established, the trend is crucial. Falling margins can be the first (and possibly the only) warning signal that a company is losing its competitive advantage.

SUMMARY

1. A competitive advantage can arise from:

   a) Top-class brand names

   b) Patents or copyrights

   c) Legal monopolies

   d) Dominance in an industry

   e) An established position in a niche market.

2. The real test of a competitive advantage is the barrier to entry into an industry. As Warren Buffett says, 'How much damage a competitor could do even if he is stupid about returns.'

3. Most growth companies are found in sectors with a tail wind behind them. Media, Pharmaceuticals and Support Services are excellent examples, in contrast to Shipbuilding, Engineering and Textiles.

4. Sector comparisons are an excellent arithmetical way of checking a company's competitive advantage. In particular, ROCE and margins can be illuminating. Most great growth stocks have a high ROCE and good margins.

5. REFS excludes intangibles when calculating ROCE. This gives a consistent basis for measuring the operating efficiency of the company's working assets.

6. To calculate ROCE, take the profit before tax, exceptional items, interest and dividends payable and express it as a percentage of the capital employed in the business, which is the sum of all ordinary and preference share capital, reserves, all classes of debt and finance lease obligations, minority interests and provisions.

7. ROCE should always be compared with the current cost of borrowing.

8. The trend of ROCE should be followed closely. A decline could indicate that a company is beginning to lose its competitive advantage.

9. REFS is examining the idea of showing Return on Investment (ROI) as an extra statistic. ROI is the rate of return that a company enjoys on the cost of invested capital.

10. Margin is another arithmetical measure of a company's competitive advantage, subject to a number of caveats:

    a) Very high margins invite competition.

b) Very low margins add to the risk of an investment.

c) Major changes in margins often occur as a result of new top management.

d) Low margin industries find it difficult to change.

e) Any significant improvement in margins is usually due to some kind of product or service enhancement, which can be identified by talking to management and studying brokers' circulars, press cuttings and the annual report.

f) A choppy record of margins usually indicates a business that is prone to periodic price wars and/or is highly cyclical.

g) The profit margins of a company should be compared with the margins of other companies in its peer group and with the sector average.

h) The trend of margins is crucial. Falling margins can be the first and only warning signal that a company is losing its competitive advantage.

10

STRONG FINANCIAL POSITION

Cash flow per share is only one measure of a company's financial strength. The level of gearing, cash balances and general liquidity are also very important indicators of its capacity to survive in difficult times.

THE GEARING RATIO

The gearing ratio is the accepted short-hand way of indicating the extent of a company's borrowings. Net gearing is calculated by taking overall borrowings, deducting cash, treasury bills and certificates of deposit, and then expressing the resultant figure as a percentage of shareholders' funds, *including intangibles* such as brand names, patents, copyrights and goodwill. Note that marketable securities are not deducted from borrowings as they may not be realisable in an emergency. Gross gearing is simply the overall borrowings of a company, without any deductions for cash and equivalents, expressed as a percentage of shareholders' funds.

REFS shows both net and gross gearing, *both including and excluding intangibles*, and indicates whether or not borrowings are repayable in under one year, under five years or, by implication, over five years. As you can see from the typical panels below, Scottish & Newcastle had net gearing of 39.5%, whereas Next had net gearing of −47.5% (48.8% cash less gross gearing of 1.36%). Expressed another way, Next's net cash per share (also shown in REFS) was 45.5p against the June 1996 share price of 564p:

SCOTTISH & NEWCASTLE			
GEARING, COVER (95AR)			
intangibles		Incl	Excl
net gearing	%	39.5	39.5
cash	%	6.55	6.55
gross gearing	%	46.0	46.0
under 5 yrs	%	39.0	39.0
under 1 yr	%	27.2	27.2
quick ratio		r	0.37
current ratio		r	0.47
interest cover		x	5.68

NEXT			
GEARING, COVER (96AR)			
intangibles		Incl	Excl
net gearing	%	−47.5	−47.5
cash	%	48.8	48.8
gross gearing	%	1.36	1.36
under 5 yrs	%	1.36	1.36
under 1 yr	%	1.36	1.36
quick ratio		r	1.62
current ratio		r	2.08
interest cover		x	356

For general guidance, gearing of over 50% might be a cause for concern, especially if a large proportion of a company's borrowings are short-term. A highly geared company is much more likely to be fully invested and committed operationally, so it is far more vulnerable than an ungeared one. In particular:

1. Any company with high gearing, which includes bank and other short-term borrowings, is likely to be very sensitive to changes in interest rates.

2. A highly geared company can be very vulnerable, and can fail completely, during a liquidity crisis, especially if most of its borrowings are short-term. There is no substitute for cash in the bank when a gale is blowing through world financial markets.

3. The results of highly geared companies tend to exaggerate the underlying trend. All shareholders' funds are invested, and further substantial borrowings result in the company being fully committed and therefore subject to prevailing winds. When businesses are recovering, high gearing can be a massive advantage for shareholders, but the reverse is also the case in tougher times.

4. A highly geared company is obviously less well equipped to deal with the unexpected, such as a major strike or a sudden recession.

As with other financial statistics, sector comparisons are of particular interest. The kinds of companies that tend to own their properties are, for example, likely to be more highly geared than those which do not require large premises or prefer to rent accommodation.

FT-SE MID 250 – HIGHEST PERCENTAGE NET GEARING

Highest percentage net borrowing-to-share capital and reserves (including intangibles)

Mkt Cap £m	Rel str 1 Mo %	Rel str 1 Yr %	Share price (p) 12 Months High	Low	Recent	Company	Last AR Net gear %	Last AR Gr gear %	Last AR Interest Cover x	Last AR Div Cover x	PCF	Last AR ROCE %
1,057	+2.9	+9.0			437	Index weighted average	27.4	59.5	42.2	2.5	5.9	31.0
569	+2.2	+2.4			345	Index median	17.8	39.3	7.9	2.4	12.9	17.5
589	−20.9	−77.9	210	64	64	Eurotunnel	458	461	0.5	na	−0.5	3.2
1,497	−2.9	+43.7	714	356	685	Danka Business Systems ...	358	575	9.3	8.9	49.1	27.7
369	+17.6	na	186	133	181	FirstBus	256	300	4.3	na	10.2	18.1
557	−4.1	+7.4	533	365	503	Flextech	238	262	−12.5	na	−29.0	−42.0
1,306	−4.5	+29.8	448	256	397	MAI	237	337	5.6	2.3	34.2	16.1
379	−5.7	−24.4	182	140	146	Man (E D & F) Group	213	246	2.3	2.2	−4.9	15.8
345	+7.3	+31.3	252	163	252	Cattles	195	202	4.8	2.0	26.9	14.9
558	+5.3	+16.1	350	257	346	Cowie Group	167	168	3.3	2.7	3.0	15.7
718	+6.0	+70.6	430	196	429	Stagecoach Holdings	150	160	4.8	3.3	8.9	18.9
1,168	−5.8	−22.1	484	377	404	Dalgety	149	171	4.9	1.5	9.2	21.1
783	+6.7	−4.1	947	792	902	Charter	117	208	5.0	2.2	19.2	13.6
466	+22.9	+48.0	688	367	667	Unitech	115	205	5.9	3.6	20.3	15.7
1,000	+9.7	+36.9	585	383	584	RJB Mining	104	106	7.6	2.0	32.1	1.8
1,354	+12.4	+31.7	656	421	656	EMAP	88.5	99.1	7.7	2.2	20.7	1255
865	+36.7	+15.9	680	489	680	South West Water	77.9	78.3	2.3	2.6	7.9	9.6
984	+25.0	+5.8	£12	840	£11.7	Securicor	74.5	83.7	12.7	9.7	52.6	23.5
885	+7.8	−20.4	444	337	392	Booker	73.5	129	4.2	1.3	6.1	26.0
366	+8.1	+12.8	459	370	456	Fine Art Developments	66.0	70.4	6.7	2.1	77.2	21.6
401	−5.9	+36.7	380	238	345	Inspec Group	65.2	80.1	11.4	3.8	18.1	28.2
528	+9.6	−24.6	58.5	21	49	Trafalgar House	64.5	148	−5.0	na	−4.0	−4.2
1,238	−0.3	−41.2	351	230	234	United Biscuits	63.8	77.8	4.5	1.6	7.0	18.1
1,598	−4.3	−30.9	963	632	715	De La Rue	62.8	119	25.9	2.5	15.5	33.3
1,254	+2.7	+14.4	940	643	814	Yorkshire Electricity	62.0	63.2	10.3	3.1	8.4	25.1
914	+6.3	−4.4	196	120	172	T & N	60.0	76.8	1.3	2.6	5.8	16.9
978	−6.4	−9.6	460	380	416	Unigate	58.4	80.8	4.4	2.0	5.8	25.0

The table above shows the 25 FT-SE Mid-250 companies with the highest net gearing on 1 April 1996. As you can see, Eurotunnel led the field with horrific gearing of 458%. There are arguments for showing gearing as a percentage of market capitalisation to eliminate anomalies, especially as nowadays so many companies have very substantial intangible assets which are not in their balance sheets. However, I prefer to use the harsher measure of comparing gearing with shareholders' funds and to check it against market value if the figure appears to be absurd.

In *The Zulu Principle* I suggested that if the gearing of a company was over 50% of net assets, it should be avoided as an investment.

Nowadays, I am much more tolerant of high gearing *provided* cash flow is really strong and gearing is being brought down rapidly. *Gearing is a trailing indicator* that is always based on last year's accounts. If the current year is progressing well and a substantial cash flow is being generated, this should be borne in mind. For example, in early 1995, the shares of Frank Usher Holdings plc were about 130p and gearing was 76% based on the figures in the annual report for the financial year ending 31 May 1994. However, cash flow in 1994 was over 16p per share with only 1p of capital expenditure. 1995 profits were forecast to be higher, so it looked as if cash flow would soon reduce gearing to a more tolerable level and the company's brokers, Credit Lyonnais Laing, forecast that gearing would be only 10% by 1997. In the event, by 31 May 1995, gearing had already been reduced to about 20%. Clearly therefore, Usher's gearing in 1994 was not a problem even though the stark figure of 76% was rather offputting at first sight.

FOUR INVESTMENT TOOLS

There are four other investment tools that I have found helpful in measuring a company's financial strength:

1. *The quick ratio* is an attempt to see what would happen if a company suddenly had to pay off all of its current liabilities. For this reason, only assets that can be readily turned into cash are included and stock and work in progress is excluded.
    The basic formula is therefore:

$$\frac{\text{Current assets less stock and work in progress}}{\text{Current liabilities}} = \text{quick ratio}$$

Generally speaking, I like to see a quick ratio of over one, but many retailing operations can manage on much less, as they can sell their products several weeks before paying their suppliers. Because of the very different circumstances of different businesses, the quick ratio of a company is best compared with the sector averages and very similar companies within the sector.
    It is important to check the quick ratio of a company when its annual report is published. If it is low in comparison with other members of the company's peer group and it is deteriorating, this can be a prelude to a fund-raising exercise.

2. *The current ratio* is similar to the quick ratio and shows the number of times current liabilities are covered by current assets. It is determined by dividing the current assets of a business (including stock and work in progress this time) by its current liabilities.

The basic formula is simply:

$$\frac{\text{Current assets}}{\text{Current liabilities}} = \text{current ratio}$$

A ratio of 2.00 or more is usually a sign of financial strength. A low ratio of under 1.25 (1.00 for retailers) can be a sign of weakness.

Also, any major fluctuations in its current ratio can alert investors to fundamental changes in a business's financial structure. Retailing companies usually have small debtors, as most of their sales are paid for in cash; they therefore usually have lower than average current ratios. In other industries, high current ratios can sometimes result from excessive stocks or poor control of debtors.

3. *Interest cover* shows the company's capacity to continue paying interest on its borrowings out of annual profits. It is calculated by taking a company's normalised historic profits *before interest and taxation* and dividing them by the annual interest charge.

This is the basic formula:

$$\frac{\text{Normalised profits before taxation and gross interest}}{\text{Annual gross interest charge}} = \text{interest cover}$$

Low and/or deteriorating interest cover is an obvious danger signal and can sometimes be a precursor to a reconstruction, fund-raising or business failure.

The REFS gearing table also highlights interest cover. As you can see, Eurotunnel appeared to be in a parlous state with its interest charges only 50% covered. In contrast, EMAP's interest charges were covered a healthy 7.7 times and Securicor's and Inspec Group's cover was into double digits.

4. *Dividend cover* shows the extent to which the historic dividend is covered by the company's earnings, ignoring the possible ACT consequences of a full distribution. It is calculated by taking a company's normalised historic earnings (or earnings per share) and

dividing them by the net dividends payable (or net dividends per share), as follows:

$$\frac{\text{Normalised historic earnings}}{\text{Net dividends payable}} = \text{Dividend cover}$$

or

$$\frac{\text{Normalised EPS}}{\text{Net dividends per share}} = \text{Dividend cover}$$

It is obviously comforting if a company's dividend is two to three times covered. However, dividend cover comes more into its own as an investment measure when the cover is very slender. In that event, there may be a cut in dividend, with disastrous consequences for the share price.

It is interesting to note that great growth companies like Rentokil, Reuters, Perpetual, Next, Eurotherm, Logica, Admiral, Parity, Druck and Halma seem to generate plenty of cash. Perhaps for this reason high gearing makes me feel ill at ease. I like companies that spit out cash regularly and preferably become awash with it. As it is possible to invest in companies which satisfy my general investment criteria and have strong cash flow and strong balance sheets into the bargain, it seems unnecessary to take an extra risk unless circumstances are very special indeed.

SUMMARY

1. Gearing of more than 50% can be a cause for concern. However, compromises can be made if cash flow is really strong and gearing is being brought down rapidly.

2. The quick ratio shows how well assets, that can be readily turned into cash, cover current liabilities. It is therefore calculated by taking current assets less stock and work in progress and dividing the result by current liabilities. Generally speaking, look for a quick ratio of more than one, but bear in mind that many retailers can operate on much less.

3. The current ratio is similar to the quick ratio but includes stock and work in progress. It will therefore always be higher than the quick ratio. A current ratio of two or more is usually a sign of financial strength.

4. Interest cover is the measure of a company's capacity to continue paying interest on its borrowings out of annual profits. Low or deteriorating interest cover can be a danger signal.

5. Dividend cover shows the extent to which historic dividend is covered, ignoring the possible ACT consequences of a full distribution.

6. Great growth companies spit out cash and usually seem to have plenty of it. As it is possible to find shares which satisfy all the growth criteria and have strong balance sheets, there is no need to take the extra risk of investing in companies with very high indebtedness, poor cash flow and weak balance sheets.

11

—

ACCELERATING EARNINGS PER SHARE

An acceleration in the rate of growth of a company's EPS often provides an excellent opportunity for buying its shares cheaply. The reason is simple – it takes a few months for the change in forecast EPS and, more importantly, the company's growth rate, to be reflected in the share price.

Take a company that is thought to be growing at 15% per annum with a share price of 172.5p – 15 times its prospective EPS of 11.5p. If brokers' forecasts were revised to anticipate a 20% growth rate in future, the share price would have a lot of work to do. First, it would have to absorb the extra 0.5p of EPS (10p growing at 15% gives the 11.5p previous forecast of EPS, so 20% would give an extra 0.5p, increasing the forecast EPS to 12p). On a maintained PER this would add 7.5p (15 times 0.5p) to the share price. However, it is likely that during the weeks that followed the announcement, the share price would rise much more dramatically. With a 20% growth rate, the PER would, on a pro-rata basis, rise from 15 to 20, so with the revised EPS of 12p, the share price would probably reach 240p. The important point to grasp is that of the increase in the share price of 67.5p only 7.5p would have resulted from the increase in EPS – the balance of 60p would have arisen from the status change in the PER.

Perhaps the most interesting point is that there is no need to speculate on whether or not a change in the EPS growth rate is about to happen. You can wait until it is a *fait accompli*. You might have to pay a little more, but if you act quickly, the major part of the status change in the PER will be yours for the taking. The market's digestive processes are so slow that it is usually still possible to buy within a week or so of the announcement of improved results and prospects.

Nevertheless, it makes sense to act as quickly as possible. Company results should therefore always be scanned closely to see if the prospect of a status change has arisen. The kind of opportunity I have in mind was well illustrated by Azlan Group, the computer software and services group that distributes Netscape's and IBM's products in Europe, when it surprised the market with a profit warning. It was the kind of profit warning that investors rarely receive – the directors announced that the forthcoming interim results, far from matching the market's expectation of £1m pre-tax, would instead be about four times greater at over £4m!

On the day before the announcement in late 1995 the shares were 350p. The day the announcement was made they rose to 420p and by early 1996 they were 600p, having also given shareholders an opportunity to buy two shares for every nine at 440p. Even at 600p, the PEG was still only 0.44, so the potential upside was very substantial. The key point that Azlan illustrates is that a share cannot absorb a large amount of good news instantly. There are always profit-takers around who are tempted when their shares rise quickly and it takes a long time for the shares to find a new level that is up with events.

In REFS, accelerating EPS can be quickly detected from the company's chart and the Earnings, Dividends Estimates panel in the company entry.

Enterprise Inns in the chart below was typical of a company with fast-decelerating EPS. In 1996, EPS were forecast to grow at over 100%, but this fell to 5.59% in 1997 as was clearly shown by the brokers' consensus forecast in the March 1996 company entry.*

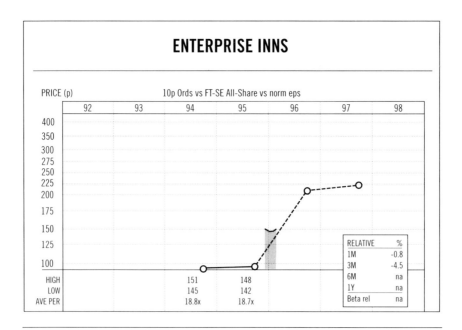

---

* In June 1996, the outlook changed completely when Enterprise Inns announced a £51.3m deal to acquire 413 pubs and a 50% share of a further 98 outlets.

Polypipe's March 1996 chart highlights that growth was continuing at a relatively steady pace. The brokers' consensus for the year ending June 1996 was for growth of 16.8% with 17.7% forecast for the following year.

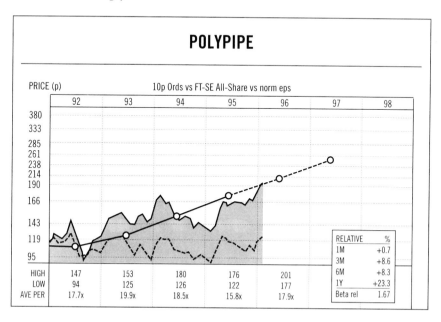

Photobition Group's chart highlights that growth in EPS was forecast to accelerate. The forecasts for the two years ending 31 March 1997, shown by the dotted line joining the three small circles, was

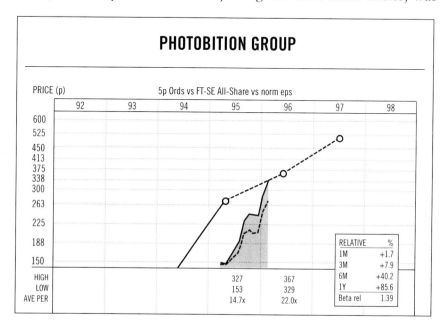

clearly sloping upward. The underlying figures showed that growth in EPS was forecast to increase to 38.3% in 1997 against 26.4% in 1996.

BROKERS' CONSENSUS FORECAST CHANGES

The other way of detecting fast-accelerating EPS is to study the REFS tables of brokers' consensus forecast changes each month.

These are presented in order of magnitude of the upward change in the current year's forecast during the previous month. They cover every index and non-index company and the top of the FT-SE SmallCap table below shows the layout. The tables for just the FT-SE SmallCap index cover about five pages and end with companies that have had their profit forecasts downgraded. The final entry is therefore for the largest percentage downward revision of the brokers' consensus forecast.

FT-SE SMALLCAP – CONSENSUS FORECAST CHANGES											
	Current year forecast			Next year forecast			Rel strength				Prosp Eps
Company	Eps p	1 Mnth Chng %	3 Mnth Chng %	Eps p	1 Mnth Chng %	3 Mnth Chng %	1 Mnth %	3 Mnth %	1 Year %	Prosp PER	Growth Rate %
Manchester United	15.4	+28.3	+28.3	21.2	+32.5	+66.9	+25.2	+90.9	+116	19.2	12.1
Alfred McAlpine	12.8	+25.5	+36.2	16.6	na	na	+9.8	+14.5	+4.8	13.5	206
Page (Michael)	21.2	+20.5	+36.8	23.4	na	na	+13.9	+32.1	+80.8	11.6	13.2
Renishaw	23.6	+18.0	+32.6	27.4	+16.6	+36.3	−4.0	+17.2	+37.2	17.9	19.8
Corporate Services	12.1	+14.9	+27.1	14.2	+21.4	na	+16.0	+47.7	+58.8	10.8	27.0
Wembley	28.2	+14.2	+14.2	29.5	na	na	+0.8	+7.2	+49.8	13.0	31.8
Servisair	12.2	+14.0	na	13.5	na	na	+2.0	+6.2	+25.8	23.3	12.8
Dewhirst Grp	14.8	+11.3	+11.3	na	na	na	−3.6	−0.3	+2.9	12.8	27.5
Psion	43.3	+10.7	+19.0	55.0	na	na	+11.7	+45.8	+195	24.1	31.4
AMEC	7.3	+10.6	+21.7	8.4	na	na	+13.6	+15.1	+40.4	15.5	−58.8
Bentalls	5.8	+9.4	+9.4	na	na	na	+14.2	+12.2	−15.2	20.0	92.1
John Laing	14.7	+8.9	+5.8	18.1	na	na	+1.6	+19.5	+29.6	20.0	3.9
Capital Industries	14.8	+8.8	na	16.2	na	na	−5.5	+2.0	+7.4	12.8	0.2
Birkby	15.2	+8.6	+7.8	15.7	na	−2.5	+0.7	−7.6	−25.5	10.5	3.3
Lamont	21.3	+8.1	+0.5	27.2	na	na	−3.2	+2.5	−28.8	12.3	9.7
Derwent Valley	12.2	+8.0	+9.9	12.3	+3.4	na	+3.0	+14.5	+23.5	30.9	5.4
Nestor-BNA	6.9	+7.8	+7.8	7.7	na	na	−3.6	+20.0	+51.4	13.8	16.5
Nichols (J N) (Vimto)	16.6	+7.8	−4.1	18.7	na	na	+0.9	−5.6	−12.3	13.0	8.5
McCarthy & Stone	5.8	+7.4	+5.5	6.9	+1.5	−4.2	+12.1	+18.2	+40.0	15.3	4.1
Asda Property	5.8	+7.4	+11.5	6.3	na	na	+1.3	+18.6	+6.9	24.3	−0.6
British-Borneo Petroleum	25.3	+6.8	−6.2	30.4	+9.8	na	−0.6	+28.8	+67.7	18.9	19.0
Peptide Therapeutics Grp	−15.3	+6.7	na	−17.4	na	na	+8.6	−0.7	na	−14.0	na
Oasis Stores	17.5	+6.1	+6.1	22.7	na	na	+34.5	+44.3	na	20.9	26.2
VCI	19.4	+6.0	+2.1	22.2	na	na	+6.4	+16.6	+65.2	16.2	13.0
Brammer	36.9	+5.4	+3.1	40.5	na	na	+0.5	+15.6	+20.3	14.2	14.4

There are a number of points to be aware of when reading the tables:

1. They focus on the change during the previous month. In some cases, this will be offset by a revision the other way during the previous three months.

2. The second set of three columns shows the next year's forecast, which is equally, if not more, important. For example, an upward revision for the current year would be uninviting if it was accompanied by an equal or greater downward revision in the following year's forecast.

3. The relative strength during the month and previous year are, as always, of vital importance.

4. The brokers' consensus forecast is, of course, usually made up of several individual forecasts. A major upward revision often follows an event such as an unexpectedly good interim or annual result, a major acquisition or divestment or a major change in the outlook for the industry. Ideally, the underlying brokers' forecasts should be checked in detail in REFS or *The Estimate Directory*. Sometimes, the consensus forecast proves to be conservative because some of the brokers are not abreast of events. The consensus in REFS is weighted in favour of recent forecasts, but if the company brokers' forecast is at a higher level than the consensus that can sometimes be encouraging.

5. The tables highlight only *possible* prospects for re-rating. Any company that appears to be attractive should always be double-checked with the company entry, the annual report, press cuttings and brokers' circulars in the usual way.

CLONING

Companies with sharply accelerating EPS often share a common feature – the capacity to clone their activities. Pelican's Café Rouge restaurants are a good example, as are JD Wetherspoon's distinctive pubs, JJB Sports' shops and Next's fashion shops.

Carpetright, which has given shareholders a joyous ride, is another company with a distinctive retailing formula. The ideal time to invest in this kind of company is when it has proved that the formula works and is beginning to roll it out.

The attraction of cloning is that the basic work of honing and refining the retailing formula only has to be done once. As soon as the formula is proven, it can be expanded nationally. As this happens, every new outlet adds to profits, central overheads usually fall as a percentage of overall costs and greater buying power enables the company to put pressure on suppliers and improve margins. It is a kind of virtuous cycle that can be very beneficial to shareholders.

The supermarkets were excellent examples of cloning in the late seventies and eighties. However, the opportunities were so great that competition became very intense and price wars flared up every few years. There are few obvious investment opportunities within the supermarkets today, with perhaps only Asda offering a slightly more innovative formula than the norm.

Investors should concentrate on identifying companies in a new field or in an attractive and distinctive extension of an existing one. New issues often highlight the opportunities. In mid-1995, for example, Oasis Stores came to the market at 148p with its small chain of women's fashion shops. Oasis seems to have found a niche for younger women, who are looking for something fashionable, not too expensive and a little different from Marks & Spencer and Next. By April 1996, Oasis shares had risen to 390p.

Another recent flotation on the AIM was Pet City, which has out-of-town supermarkets for everything to do with pets. I visited the Edinburgh branch one Sunday in early 1996 and found it very crowded and obviously doing well. However, Pet City is not forecasting profits for some time to come. In cases like these, I prefer to sit on the fence until the financial results are to hand and are obviously inviting.

The key point to understand is that there is usually plenty of time to climb aboard excellent situations. For example, in late 1995, the share price of JJB Sports had already increased by 170% since flotation in late 1994. Even then at 575p,* the prospective year-ahead price-earnings ratio was only 15 – about the same as the average of the market. The average company was forecast to increase its EPS by only 10% in the year ahead, but JJB's had been growing at over 50% for five years and was forecast to grow at about 30%.

In January 1996, JJB announced that overall sales for the 47 weeks ended 24 December 1995 were up over 50% and, most importantly,

---

*There was a 2 for 1 bonus issue in June 1996.

that like-for-like sales were up an astonishing 17.8%. The company also announced that contracts had been exchanged for seven new high street stores and 15 further out-of-town superstores to be opened in 1996.

JJB's announcement contained a very important message that should always be checked. It is all very well to increase sales by buying or opening new stores, but the key to the future success of a retailing operation that is being cloned is whether or not existing branches are also improving. The magic words are 'like-for-like sales' – when they start to falter it is time to wave goodbye to the company.

Companies that can successfully clone their activities often command substantial PERs. This is especially true in America, where multiples are sometimes as high as 50, and over 30 is commonplace. The main reason is that the American home market is vast and good retailing concepts can be rolled out perhaps five or six times more than in the UK. In America, investors are used to super-growth and are prepared to pay for it. In the UK, investors are distrustful of companies growing at an exceptional rate, so it is often easy to buy shares in these kinds of companies at bargain prices in relation to their growth prospects.

It is important not to pay too high a multiple – my limit is usually 20 prospective. After a few years the PER is bound to regress to the norm and its fall must be amortised over the period of the investment. Harry Ramsden, for example, has a very successful formula with its classy fish and chip restaurants, which it can clone for many years to come, both in the UK and abroad. However, perhaps on takeover prospects, the multiple in May 1996 was already in the high thirties compared with a growth rate in the low twenties. Although Harry Ramsden had great growth prospects, the arithmetic appeared to me to be unattractive.

SUMMARY

1. Fast accelerating EPS growth takes time to be reflected in a share price, while the growing EPS are absorbed into the price arithmetically and the improved PER (due to the higher growth rate) multiplies the increased figure.

2. The graphs in REFS highlight the trend of EPS growth. The dotted line joining the EPS estimates slopes sharply upward for accelerating EPS and downward for decelerating EPS.

3. The monthly tables of brokers' consensus forecast changes in REFS are an ideal way of detecting those companies with fast increasing or faltering EPS growth rates.

4. If possible, underlying brokers' forecasts should be checked and, in particular, the company broker's forecast, which is likely to be the most reliable.

5. Sharply accelerating EPS growth often arises when a company has developed a successful formula that can be cloned.

6. New issues (shown in the non-index tables of REFS) are a good hunting ground for young companies with a formula that can be cloned.

7. Always keep a keen eye on like-for-like sales. If these begin to falter, the company may be running into too much competition.

8. Avoid companies with a cloning formula but no profits and those that are on *prospective* multiples of over 20. If you overpay for future growth your eventual rewards will be that much smaller.

12

—

OTHER INVESTMENT CRITERIA

SMALL MARKET CAPITALISATION

In *The Zulu Principle*, I coined the expression 'elephants don't gallop'. It is obviously far easier for a management team to double the size of a company capitalised at £10m than one worth £1bn. From an investor's point of view, an attractive range is between £30m and £250m.

Over the last 50 years or so, small companies have outperformed the market by about 3.8%, but they are often out of favour for several years at a stretch. The main disadvantage of small companies is that they lack marketability and therefore do not appeal to many of the institutions. For private investors, with only a few thousand shares to buy in each company, getting in and out is usually not so much of a problem, but for institutions, with hundreds of thousands of shares, it can be a very different matter.

Even private investors need to be careful when investing in small companies, the prices of which can come under pressure if market-makers suddenly find themselves with too much stock when the market's mood turns bearish. Not only can a share price fluctuate violently, but market-makers' spreads often become massive. REFS shows the number of shares that market-makers are happy to deal in next to the price, marked with the letters NMS (Normal Market Size). Three noughts need to be added to the REFS figure so 3, for example, would indicate a normal market size of 3,000 shares.

I deal in relatively large quantities compared with most private investors. When I am buying, I am usually prepared to pay a little more to obtain the number of shares I am looking for and when I have to sell, I am equally prepared to take a small discount if necessary. If the original investment is well conceived, the potential profits are usually sufficient to carry the extra cost of dealing in small companies.

AIM

In mid-1996, there were about 200 companies quoted on the Alternative Investment Market (AIM). The largest was Trocadero, capitalised at £350m, Southern Newspapers was second at £140m and Pet City Holdings was third at £98m. The smallest AIM company was Silkbam, capitalised at only £58,000 and there were 15 companies capitalised at under £2m.

I very rarely deal in AIM stocks as most of them are not sufficiently marketable for my purposes and there are very few brokers' forecasts. My advice to most private investors is to invest in AIM stocks only if they believe that they know something truly special about a particular company.

FLEDGLING INDEX

The Fledgling index, excluding investment trusts, is made up of about 700 companies with market capitalisations ranging up to almost £100m. In June 1996, companies of this size, like Regal Hotel Group and Tottenham Hotspur, were becoming candidates for promotion to the FT-SE SmallCap index.

As the name implies, the Fledgling index contains a large number of companies that are learning to fly. Unfortunately, it also contains an equally large number with broken wings. In early 1996, it was interesting to note that within the Fledgling index only 60 companies had PEGs. This was mainly due to the index being the dustbin that collects the failures demoted from the other indices, and the companies that never really get off the ground.

Unless you know something very special about a fledgling company, it should be treated warily. Generally speaking, look for companies with at least two brokers making profit forecasts, with a low standard deviation between them. Also try to make sure that the marketability is enough to handle the size of your investment with relative ease and that the market-makers' spread is not too wide. If, for example, a share price is 100–110p and the price rises to 140–150p, an investor will only enjoy the 30p difference (after brokerage) between the buying price of 110p and the selling price of 140p. This is a massive potential levy on future profit and needs to be borne in mind at the time of purchase.

FT-SE SMALLCAP INDEX

The FT-SE SmallCap index contains about 400 shares with market capitalisations in June 1996 ranging from Wilshaw at £33m to Serco at over £330m. It is an ideal hunting ground for shares with attractive PEGs. The companies in the index are sizeable enough to be more secure than fledgling companies, they are usually followed by more than one broker, are more marketable and are often still at the stage when their primary core businesses have a lot of growth left in them. Companies like JJB Sports, rolling out its successful formula for sports shops, and Pizza Express, with its pizza restaurants, illustrate this well. In both cases, they should be able to treble their coverage of the UK before they near saturation point. In contrast, a very successful company like Next (now a FT-SE 100 company) can no longer hope to open many more UK branches and therefore has to rely on further growth from existing branches which, in many cases, are being upgraded. Further scope for super-growth may, of course, come from overseas expansion but that, in turn, usually carries greater risks.

THE MID-250 INDEX

As the name implies, the Mid-250 index covers 250 companies with market capitalisations in June 1996 ranging from Wickes at £260m to Lucas at just over £2bn. In the eight six-month periods tested so far, the PEG formula has been successful with companies in the Mid-250 index. In thirteen six-month tests in 1995/6, using just one sieve, a PEG cut-off of 0.75, the Mid-250 index average performance of 9.56% was beaten by the low PEG average of 14.88%.

Although this is a significantly improved performance, it is not so impressive as low PEG shares in the FT-SE 100 and in the FT-SE SmallCap indices. In the Mid-250 index, there seems to be a dearth of growth companies still concentrating on the unfulfilled growth in their core activities. There have been some spectacular successes, such as Stagecoach, Sage and Carpetright, for example, but there are very few other companies that have performed outstandingly well. It is possible that the pendulum will swing in the Mid-250's favour in future tests and certainly REFS will be keeping the test results under active review every month.

FT-SE 100 INDEX

The FT-SE 100 index does, of course, cover the leading 100 companies in the UK. In June 1996, the market capitalisations ranged from British Petroleum's £31bn to Lasmo's £1.7bn. The FT-SE 100 index stocks have the great advantage of being highly marketable. Overseas investors are attracted to them as they tend to be the only companies that they have heard about. Also tracker funds are obliged to buy them.

Because of the advantage of better marketability, investors can relax their normal criteria a little. For example, for a FT-SE 100 index stock, it would be perfectly reasonable to buy on a PEG of 0.75 instead of my normal limit of about 0.6. It is in fact necessary to lower the standard to obtain a worthwhile universe of shares to invest in. In mid-1995, for example, only five shares would have qualified with a PEG of under 0.75, but they would have beaten the market by a very wide margin. The FT-SE 100 index shares with a PEG cut-off of 0.75 have been back-tested since the inception of REFS. In thirteen tests of six-month periods since November 1994, shares with PEGs of under 0.75 have risen by an average of 21.04% against only 9.53% for the average of the FT-SE 100 index.

NON-INDEX

REFS also provides monthly company entries for non-index companies and shows monthly tables of non-index companies with the lowest PEGs, highest growth rates and the like. At the beginning of each year, most of these companies are promoted to an index, usually the Fledgling. As the year progresses, new issues add to the slender universe of non-index shares until the tables become quite substantial.

The non-index tables are another excellent hunting ground for growth shares with low PEGs. New issues often take several months to be fully appreciated by the market and as non-index shares are promoted to the various indices, they are often helped on their way by tracker funds which are compelled to buy them.

ATTRACTIVE DIVIDEND YIELDS

In itself, a substantial dividend yield is of no real importance to a growth investor. Warren Buffett always argues that retained earnings can be of greater benefit to shareholders, as growth companies use the money for expansion and usually make an excellent return on capital.

Arguably, the funds that could have been used to pay extra dividends are far better employed in the company's hands than they would be by the shareholders themselves.

However, an attractive dividend yield helps to support a share price. It tends to come into play more with asset situations than with growth stocks. Most investors prefer growth stocks to pay dividends, even if they are small. There are some funds that do not invest in companies unless they pay dividends, and it is always nice to know that institutions are not precluded from investing. It might be their money that buys your shares, when you wish to head for the exit.

Another reason for favouring dividend-paying companies is that the level of the interim and final dividend payments can provide a valuable guide to the directors' confidence in the trading outlook. For example, if a company with a history of dividend payments increasing year after year suddenly fails to increase the dividend one year, or substantially reduces the percentage rate of increase, that might be a warning signal.

There are several successful share systems based simply on buying shares with high yields. The most noteworthy is that of Michael O'Higgins outlined in his excellent book *Beating the Dow* and applied to the UK in my book *PEP Up Your Wealth*. The companies highlighted by this kind of system are, however, frequently in distress and their dividend yield is sometimes the only support for the share price. Growth investors can afford to have a very different approach. They should not worry unduly about the percentage yield, but they should give mild preference to companies that have a record of paying increasing dividends over several years, with further increases forecast for the year ahead.

A COMPANY BUYING IN ITS OWN SHARES

It is usually a very bullish sign when a company announces that it intends to buy in its own shares and confirms this by beginning to do so.

First, it shows the confidence of the board in the company and it usually implies that the company's liquidity is strong.

Second, the supply of the company's stock is tightened as shares overhanging the market are mopped up and cancelled by the buying programme.

Third, buying in shares is usually earnings-enhancing. Take, for example, a company on a prospective PER of 14 – its earnings *after tax* represent about 7% of the share price and before tax about 10.5%. In other words, for an asset to pay its way in group terms it has to produce a return of at least 10.5%. In mid-1996, the most that a company might have earned in interest on its surplus cash would be about 5% before tax. The extra 5.5% achieved by reducing both the cash pile and the number of shares in issue can represent a significant earnings enhancement.

There is a further reason for liking companies that buy in their shares. It shows that the directors are shareholder-conscious and are thinking along the right lines.

Warren Buffett advocates that companies with surplus cash should consider returning it to shareholders. Buying in shares by a general offer is an attractive way of doing this as it allows those shareholders who prefer to continue enjoying the ride to retain their shares and those who want to take some profits to sell some of their holding.

The fact that a company is buying in its own shares is not an automatic buying signal for investors. However, it is undoubtedly a very strong point to weigh up when making a final decision – very similar in many ways to a number of directors buying shares.

SOMETHING NEW

'Something new' can often be a good reason to buy a company's shares. The something in question usually falls into one of four categories:

1. New management

2. New technology or new products

3. New events in the industry as a whole, including new legislation

4. New acquisitions

New management has already been considered on pages 77–8 under the heading of Chief Executive Officer Changes.

New products or new technology are very well illustrated by Psion with its revolutionary palm-top computer, which has helped to transform the company. I first recommended the shares at 100p in the *Financial Mail on Sunday* in 1992, when the company still had worrying teething troubles with its new computer. It was clear then that if the problems could be solved, the prospects would be excellent. By May 1996, the problems were a distant memory and Psion's shares stood at 1300p.

REFS subscribers would have noticed Psion in the PEG tables in May 1995, when the company's management had begun to prove itself and the shares were priced at 323p with a PEG of 0.64. They could have bought them then with comparative safety and made a very substantial gain. Provided you are right, *speculating* on whether or not management will solve major problems is obviously very much more rewarding than *investing* when the management has already done so. If you are wrong, however, you can lose most of your money.

A company like Memory, with its technique for repairing computer chips, is hoping for massive future profits, but has yet to deliver. In this book, the emphasis is on growth companies with established records with at least four years of consecutive EPS growth, whether it be historic or forecast or a combination of the two. Investors following this methodology are not interested in shares valued on a wing and a prayer – they will be waiting for evidence in the shape of fast-growing EPS. Although the early large gains from taking a punt are missed this way, there is usually still plenty of time to climb aboard at a later stage.

New events in an industry would include happenings as diverse as the discovery of oil in the North Sea, changes in the law relating to television licences, the collapse of a major competitor in an industry or the opening of the Channel Tunnel. An armistice with the IRA would obviously benefit restaurants and hotels in London and, in contrast, a major increase in the price of oil could affect airline profits adversely. It is important for investors to be aware of these kinds of events as they can have a very definite impact on share prices.

New acquisitions also have a major effect on shares. When Hanson acquired Imperial Tobacco, it lifted the company's stature, making it overnight an important part of the fabric of British industry. On a much smaller scale, Wassall's acquisition of General Cable in America was a bold and attractive acquisition, which had a major impact on Wassall's share price as the potential began to be realised.

An important point to consider with any acquisitions funded by a share exchange is the potential dilution of EPS and the impact of the extra shares being put on the market. Sometimes, the market can take a long time to absorb a major increase in share capital.

A very important feature of any acquisition is that it should be earnings-enhancing, at least in the longer term. The market does not like earnings-dilutive acquisitions, as was demonstrated with Farnell Electronics, when it acquired the American company Premier on a much higher multiple than its own. Farnell may still prove that the acquisition will be earnings-enhancing in the longer run, but the management has an uphill task and a lot of work to do to claw back the dilution in EPS as a result of the share issue.

To my mind, the best kinds of acquisitions are the small and juicy ones in fragmented industries that almost pass unnoticed. I have in mind companies like Photobition, which makes three or four acquisitions of competitive businesses every year. It often absorbs the turnover into its own business, sells off the property and saves most of the overheads. These kinds of aquisitions often go unnoticed but, cumulatively, they have a very significant impact on future EPS growth.

To summarise, 'something new' is not a reason in itself for buying a share. The fundamentals need to be right too but, if they are, something new can be a very attractive bonus and is often the reason behind the hopes for rapidly improving EPS.

PRICE-TO-SALES RATIO

Jim O'Shaughnessy's recent research into the S & P CompuStat database has shown that a price-to-sales ratio (PSR) of under 1.0, coupled with high relative strength in the previous twelve months, has been one of the most potent combinations of investment criteria over the last 43 years. His argument is backed up by Kenneth Fisher, who explains in his book *Super Stocks* how effective a low PSR can be in valuing technology stocks that have experienced a major setback (see Chapter 17).

The PSR is calculated by dividing the company's market capitalisation by its total sales, excluding VAT. This is the same as dividing the company's share price by the company's sales per share.

The PSR is mainly used to spot recovery situations or to double-check that a growth company is not becoming overvalued. It is particularly useful when a company begins to make losses and, as a result, has no PER with which to value the shares. Often a company in trouble will also lose its dividend yield. The PSR is then one of the few remaining measures for valuing the business. All things being equal, a low PSR (high sales in relation to the market capitalisation) is good news for investors, and a very high PSR can be a warning signal.

Needless to say, turnover is only valuable to a business if it can eventually be converted into profit. Construction companies, for example, report very high turnover, but, except in building booms, rarely make much profit. Profit margins, the trend of margins and sector comparisons should, therefore, be studied in conjunction with PSR statistics. Sector comparisons often reveal interesting anomalies and investment opportunities in particular industries.

Another important and variable factor is the level of a company's debt. A company with no debt and a low PSR is clearly a better proposition than a company with very high debt and the same PSR. At some time in the future, the debt will need to be repaid and further equity will almost certainly need to be issued. The extra shares will then have to be added to the market capitalisation, increasing the PSR of the company in question. For this reason, the REFS tables of shares with low PSRs always show the gearing of each company alongside its PSR.

It follows that gearing should be at reasonable levels to make PSR comparisons valid. Otherwise notional allowances need to be made to allow for the likely issue of further equity. The method of calculating the allowances would, of course, have to be consistent between the companies compared, but certainly the PSR should not be taken at its face value for a company that is very highly geared.

Take a simple example of a company which had an attractive PSR. In March 1991, Next had a market capitalisation, based on a price of

30p, of £100m and sales of £400m. The PSR was therefore a stunning 0.25, £100m÷£400m, so it is not such a great surprise that, by May 1996, with new management, the share price had recovered to 530p.

It is interesting to note that Next still had a very low PSR even after the sale of Grattan, when it had eliminated most of its debt and some kind of recovery was foreseeable. Prior to that, in December 1990, its market capitalisation had slumped to £24m against forecast sales, including Grattan, of £800m. The PSR was then an astonishing .03, although, at that stage, recovery was much more difficult to foresee.

For value investors, a PSR of 0.5 or under indicates that substantial value could be present and gives an idea of the scope of a possible future recovery. For growth investors, a PSR of under one is of primary interest as a value filter. If all the other criteria such as a low PEG, strong cash flow and high relative strength are in place, a low PSR is a kind of added bonus.

It is not difficult to find shares that combine all of these characteristics. For example, in March 1996, Ideal Hardware, Parity, MITIE, Sanderson Electronics and Pressac fitted the bill.

Ideal Hardware illustrated an important point. It is a distributor operating with comparatively small margins, so it is not surprising that its PSR was on the low side. This emphasises again how important it is to check the PSR of a company against other companies in its peer group and against the sector average.

It should be borne in mind that a low PSR is not a mandatory requirement for a growth company. Great growth stocks often have massive PSRs and maintain them for years. For example, in March 1996, Rentokil, a classic growth stock, had a PSR of 4.80 with margins of 24% compared with only 1.07 and 5.97% for BET at the Rentokil bid price. It is easy to imagine how much Rentokil's management were looking forward to getting their hands on BET and improving its margins.

SUMMARY

1. Companies with a small market capitalisation in the region of £30m – 250m are more likely to outperform the market as a whole and are certainly more likely to perform better than their elephantine brethren in the FT-SE 100 index. The successful ones are often helped on their way by tracker funds, as they are promoted to higher indices.

2. Companies paying dividends are to be preferred. Dividends widen the universe of potential buyers of the shares and are a further guide to the directors' confidence or otherwise about the future.

3. When a company buys in its own shares, this is usually a very bullish sign. It shows confidence and implies that the company's liquidity is strong. Also, buying in shares tightens the supply of a company's stock and is usually earnings enhancing.

4. Something new is an attractive bonus factor. It may arise from new management, new technology, new events in an industry or new acquisitions.

5. A low price-to-sales ratio is an attractive investment feature. The level of a company's gearing should be taken into account when comparing its PSR with that of other companies.

    The nature of a company's business is also a critical factor. Distributors, for example, with low margins, tend to have low PSRs.

    Many great growth companies maintain high PSRs for years. A low PSR is not mandatory for a growth share; it is a value characteristic that is an added attraction.

13

—

YOUR STOCKBROKER
AND YOU

An important decision to be made by most private investors is whether or not they should use an execution-only broker or a broker with a more traditional and helpful service. There is no doubt that using an execution-only broker saves commission, but many investors like to obtain a second opinion and to have their hand held to a certain extent.

If you intend to use an execution-only broker, Fidelity and Sharelink are two of the largest and best-known, although by no means the cheapest. Fidelity Brokerage is the UK stockbroking arm of Boston-based Fidelity Investments. Fidelity does not leave you completely on your own, as it provides a broad range of market and company information free of charge. However, they will definitely expect you to make your own decisions, and thereby save commission. In broad terms, Fidelity's charges are about 50% of those of a traditional broker for small clients.

Sharelink's charges are about the same as Fidelity's. However, they also have a Sharefinder service, which covers the leading 650 companies. It has three essential features – a weekly performance summary, a weekly buy/sell guide and individual company reports. There are modest charges for these extra services but they seem to be good value.

Other execution-only services which appear to offer attractive commission rates include City Deal Services, a member of the Cater Allen group, which will buy or sell £1,000 worth of shares for as little as £9, and YorkShare, the Yorkshire Building Society's share dealing service, whose charges are broadly similar. Both also offer PEPs and other services, such as bed-and-breakfast deals at the end of the tax year.

All these execution-only brokers advertise regularly in magazines such as *Investors Chronicle*, and are happy to send brochures if you call them. Their contact numbers are: Fidelity – 0800 222 150; Sharelink – 0121 200 2242; YorkShare – 01274 736736; City Deal Services – 01708 738688.

Traditional brokers' commissions on the purchase and sale of stocks range from about 1.65% to less than 0.3% according to the size of the transaction and the importance of the client. You should not begrudge a good broker his commission provided you get the right level of service. You should be looking for a broker who is really switched on and anxious to please.

Many small investors feel that they cannot be too demanding because their account is relatively small and therefore unimportant to their broker. This is where REFS comes to the rescue by sieving out companies that would otherwise waste subscribers' time and the time of their broker. It helps to conserve energy by quickly eliminating those companies that are not worth pursuing, thereby enabling you to concentrate your research on those that stand a really good chance of becoming a part of your portfolio. If a company's cash flow is well below its EPS or its previous year's relative strength is poor, or its PEG is over one – give it a miss. There will be enough shares that fulfill all of your criteria, so do not waste your time, and your broker's, in obtaining further information about shares which are unlikely to be of much interest in the final analysis.

The minimum information you will require to check out a share will be the last two annual and interim reports and press cuttings for the previous six months. The last three annual reports would be preferable and twelve months' press cuttings, but that might be asking for too much if you are going to be checking companies every week. To save troubling your broker unduly, it is preferable to fax the company secretary of the company in question to request annual and interim reports. They are usually very obliging and REFS always gives the fax number in the company entry.

I always ask my broker to try to get hold of other brokers' circulars on any company in which I am interested – the more of them you can read the better.

Whether you invest or not, it pays to make a file on each company. You will often find that you return to them a year or so later and it would be a pity to have to start all over again. Needless to say, if you do invest, or are likely to do so, the file should be kept up to date.

Before making a final investment decision, the REFS entry should be checked in great detail, together with directors' dealings and the company's position in its sector. A wide range of factors and ratios need to be weighed up and in the next chapter I will show you how to draw all the strands together.

14

—

PUTTING IT ALL TOGETHER

The preceding chapters have covered a large number of investment criteria for selecting growth shares. Some are mandatory, others are highly desirable and the remainder can best be looked upon as attractive bonuses. As a first step, I will list all of the criteria and group them into categories:

A. MANDATORY

1. *A PEG*

Less than half of the shares in the FT-SE All-Share index have a PEG, so if a company has been awarded one it is an immediate and major plus point. It at least means that the company has a four-year pattern of growth, even if future prospects need to be combined with the past record to achieve that minimum requirement.

A compromise can sometimes be made when it is *obvious* that a company will have a PEG within a year or has just missed having one by a whisker. In most cases, however, an existing PEG is essential.

In *The Zulu Principle,* I suggested, as a mandatory requirement, that the chairman's statement should be optimistic. The fact that a company possesses a PEG provides some assurance that brokers believe there is unlikely to be a setback in EPS growth. However, any statement on future prospects in the annual report or the chairman's comments at the AGM (both synopsised in REFS) should still be checked together with newsflow to ensure that no clouds are lurking on the horizon.

A PEG cut-off level has to be established in relation to the market average. In April 1996, the market as a whole was on a PEG of about 1.5, which was historically quite high. In that climate, any share with a PEG of under 1.0 was superficially a very attractive investment. A PEG of 0.75 was twice as attractive as the market as a whole and the few shares with PEGs of under 0.6 were 2.5 times as appealing.

The level of PEG cut-off varies with the size of funds under management. A cut-off of 0.6, with other sieves, often results in a universe of only ten companies, which is sufficient for most private investors. For really significant funds, a PEG of under 1.0 would be a good starting point and should result in a much wider universe, with some of the companies in question being in the highly marketable FT-SE 100 index and a substantial number in the Mid-250.

2. *A prospective PER of not more than 20*

To command a low and attractive PEG, a share with a PER of over 20 would require a very high and probably unsustainable rate of future growth. The most reliable and recommended range of PERs and growth rates is a prospective PER of 10–20 with a forecast growth rate of 15–30%.

3. *Strong cash flow*

As you will have seen, the cash flow sieve has not, as yet, resulted in improved performance. However, it is reassuring to nervous investors (I put myself in this category) and may well come into its own in a bear market.

For my money, strong cash flow is essential. I want to see EPS converted into cash year after year and to see it translating into strong cash balances or, at the very least, rapidly reducing gearing. Cash flow per share for the last reported year should exceed EPS. Sometimes a compromise can be made if the difference is mildly negative, provided that there is a good reason (e.g. very rapidly increasing sales with a consequent increase in working capital). However, if the last reported one-year figure is adverse, the average cash flow per share for the previous five years must substantially exceed EPS for that period.

Also, capital expenditure should not exceed cash flow for the latest year and should, on average, be significantly less over the preceding five. Again, a compromise can sometimes be made for the latest year, if there is a good explanation.

Ideally, though, one is looking for companies that generate plenty of cash and do not need to spend it all on capital expenditure just to stay alive.

4. *Low gearing or positive cash*

When gearing exceeds 50%, caution is needed. In practice, I am prepared to increase this limit to about 75%, provided cash flow is strong. For example, Frank Usher Holdings had gearing of over 75% in early 1995, but by April 1996 it had been reduced to 25%.

Positive cash balances remain one of the best signs of a great growth company. In June 1996, Rentokil, Next, Carpetright, Eurotherm, Logica, Parity and JJB Sports, for example, all shared this endearing characteristic. A strong cash balance is often the most convincing evidence that a company's growth is real and that it can convert its increasing EPS into cash. This is essential to fund capital expenditure and acquisitions, buy in shares or pay increasing dividends to shareholders.

5. *High relative strength*

Relative share price strength in the previous month must be positive and relative strength in the previous twelve months must be both positive and greater than the one-month figure.

The only compromise I recommend is on the relative strength of the previous month, which may sometimes be mildly negative while a great growth share pauses for breath. In this event, I check the relative strength for the previous three months. If that is negative too, I give the shares a miss and look elsewhere.

6. *Competitive advantage*

I usually find the shares I invest in by beginning with the whole universe of quoted shares and applying a series of sieves like low PEGs, strong cash flow and high relative strength. I then examine the shares that find their way through the sieves and try to identify the competitive advantage that they must be enjoying to possess such outstanding financial characteristics. In late 1995, my sieves helped me to find Forth Ports and

Rutland Trust. The common feature of these two companies is that they both own ports. I had never given much thought to ports before, but it now seems obvious that, like toll bridges, they have a strong competitive advantage in their local area. I can therefore understand why the financial results of these companies were so good and their prospects looked so bright.

I can see that JJB Sports with its sports shops, Carpetright with its carpet stores and Pizza Express with its restaurants all have an attractive formula that they can clone. However, I found them by using REFS and arithmetical sieves. Only then did I try to check their competitive advantage to understand how they had been able to produce such good results.

Chapter 9 highlighted the many different types of competitive advantage that can be the source of a company's winning formula. High ROCE and good operating margins are usually strong supportive evidence of a company's competitive advantage.

7. *Directors' dealings*

I would be distinctly put off a share if a number of directors were actively reducing their shareholdings. Buying by directors is highly desirable, but it is not essential. The absence of *major* selling *is* mandatory.

B. HIGHLY DESIRABLE

1. *Accelerating EPS*

This is one of the most encouraging of all indicators, especially if the source (e.g. cloning) can be identified and looks like continuing.

2. *Directors buying*

A cluster of directors buying is always very encouraging.

3. *Market capitalisation*

My preferred range is £30m to £250m.

4. *Dividend yield*

Preference should be given to companies that are paying dividends. Most of them do, and those that do not should be treated with caution.

C. BONUS FACTORS

1. *A low price-to-sales ratio (PSR)*

A low PSR is an excellent value filter that can be applied to growth shares, to give added reassurance.

2. *Something new*

A change of CEO, new products or a major acquisition can have a significant effect on future EPS and can often be the trigger for a reappraisal of a company's PER.

3. *A low price-to-research ratio (PRR)*

The PRR is only a useful measure for companies which engage as a way of life in a substantial amount of research and development each year. REFS shows PRRs in company entries when there has been R and D expenditure of over 1% of market capitalisation as shown by the company's latest annual report.

The PRR is calculated by dividing the market capitalisation of a company by the total of R and D expenditure. In pharmaceuticals and computer software companies it is always encouraging to see a low PRR indicating that a substantial amount is being invested in the future of the company. More of this in Chapter 17.

4. *Reasonable asset position*

This is a low priority for growth shares and is only of any real significance if the company's gearing is high.

USING THE QUIVER FULL OF ARROWS

I like to think of all these criteria as a quiver full of arrows. They do not all need to be fired and some may miss the target. The best way to show you how to use them is to give some practical real-life examples. I would like to stress that any shares mentioned by name are for illustrative purposes only and are not to be taken as current recommendations. I will work from REFS' December issue dated 27 November 1995 as, by the time this book is published, it will be very much out of date. It is the approach that you should concentrate upon, not the companies used to illustrate it.

The FT-SE SmallCap index is a wonderful hunting ground for finding shares with attractive PEGs, so my first thought on receiving REFS each month is to turn to the table of SmallCap growth shares with the lowest PEGs. Set out below is the top part of the SmallCap table showing the shares with PEGs of under 0.6 on 27 November 1995:

FT-SE SMALLCAP – LOWEST PEGs FOR GROWTH COMPANIES

Growth companies with lowest price-earnings growth factors based on consensus forecast eps for the 12 months ahead.

Mkt Cap £m	1 Mo Rel Str %	Share price (p) 12 Months			Company	Prosp PEG	Prosp PER	Prosp Eps Growth Rate %	3-Year Eps Growth Rate %	Fcast 1 Mnth Chng %	1 Yr Rel Str %	Last AR Cflow/ Eps ratio x
		High	Low	Recent								
160	−2.5			283	Index weighted average	1.05	22.3	26.6	29.3	−3.8	+0.4	1.6
93	−3.8			183	Index median	1.01	12.5	13.6	16.9	−0.6	−12.3	1.3
50	−4.2	499	330	485	Norbain	0.37	16.7	44.7	63.2	na	−1.7	na
40	−7.6	110	80	89	Yorkshire Food Group	0.39	6.6	17.0	6.7	+1.7	−33.3	na
74	−3.5	109	70	103	Pelican Group	0.40	12.4	31.0	17.8	na	−3.1	1.6
39	−8.2	166	124	156	Perry	0.41	8.3	20.1	28.9	+0.6	−18.9	1.1
130	−5.1	303	221	289	British-Borneo	0.43	10.0	23.1	3.1	+2.6	+13.3	2.5
65	−5.0	206	152	190	Sanderson Bramall	0.46	9.1	19.8	27.1	na	−1.3	0.6
74	+4.3	175	106	175	Parity	0.49	13.9	28.7	24.2	na	+17.6	1.4
305	−1.2	131	63	130	Ashley (Laura)	0.49	34.0	69.7	152	na	+39.4	4.0
208	−1.4	96.5	51.9	95	Mayflower Corp	0.49	15.4	31.2	31.4	na	+55.1	0.3
100	−17.1	156	108	109	Vardon	0.50	10.8	21.7	96.0	+1.2	−23.1	1.5
82	−3.2	356	224	324	Delphi Grp	0.54	11.2	20.8	57.8	+1.6	+19.3	na
181	+0.4	361	173	361	Business Post Group	0.54	17.4	32.1	50.7	+0.6	+98.5	1.2
171	−7.3	217	145	193	Hogg Robinson	0.56	9.4	16.9	5.1	na	−18.9	1.3
159	−7.3	362	257	341	Independent Insurance	0.57	6.6	11.5	na	−0.2	+20.3	na
201	−2.1	269	198	214	Frost Group	0.58	13.0	22.6	30.8	−0.7	−15.9	2.2
99	+5.8	41	25	40	Rutland Trust	0.58	13.6	23.3	0.4	−4.0	+27.8	5.0
94	+1.8	604	307	599	Regent Inns	0.58	16.7	28.6	48.3	+1.5	+70.8	0.6
198	−8.7	482	346	437	Brammer	0.59	12.3	20.7	13.9	+1.0	+9.8	1.5
41	−3.5	131	106	111	Hill & Smith	0.60	9.6	16.0	3.6	na	−26.1	1.0
125	−3.5	274	151	266	Vardy (Reg)	0.60	12.2	20.3	31.0	na	+43.5	0.8
186	+5.3	373	324	361	Trinity Holdings	0.61	14.4	23.6	40.3	na	−2.3	0.7
90	−1.6	110	78.5	106	Aberdeen Trust	0.61	14.5	23.7	66.5	na	+17.4	1.3
99	−1.2	798	625	798	Admiral	0.62	15.9	25.8	13.9	+0.3	+6.1	1.1
216	+0.2	110	81.5	110	Singer & Friedlander	0.62	9.2	14.8	na	−1.9	+15.0	na
99	_8.6	174	110	161	Page (Michael)	0.65	10.5	16.1	43.3	−0.7	+20.7	1.9

It is essential to realise that, just by possessing a PEG, every share in the table has already passed through an important first sieve. Only 160 companies qualifed out of the 400 in the SmallCap index and only 20 of those passed through a second sieve and had a PEG of 0.6 or under.

The third sieve eliminated those shares from the top 20 with cash flow less than their EPS. This ratio is shown clearly in the last column of the table and, as you can see, Norbain, Yorkshire Food, Sanderson Bramall, Mayflower, Delphi Group, Regent Inns (a sad loss) and Reg Vardy failed to qualify. You will notice that Independent Insurance remained in the shortlist. The cash flow sieve is waived for banks and insurance companies, because management of cash is their line of business, so REFS does not show the figures, as they tend to be relatively meaningless.

The fourth important sieve is relative strength for the previous year. Pelican Group, Perry, Vardon (bingo interests suffering from the lottery), Hogg Robinson, Frost Group (garages suffering from the petrol price wars), and Hill & Smith were all eliminated.

As a result, the shortlist was reduced to the following shares: British-Borneo Petroleum, Parity, Laura Ashley, Business Post Group, Independent Insurance, Rutland Trust and Brammer.

The further sieve of relative strength during the previous month is less important than over a year so it can be overridden by positive relative strength in the previous three months. BritishBorneo's −5.1% was +3.5% over three months and Laura Ashley's −1.2% was +16.2%. However, regrettably, Independent Insurance's −7.3% was still negative at −2.9% and Brammer's −8.7% also stayed negative at −3.8%.

The shortlist was therefore reduced to the following shares:

	p
British-Borneo Petroleum	289
Parity	175
Laura Ashley	130
Business Post Group	361
Rutland Trust	40

We now need to look at the individual company entries in REFS, the annual reports and any available brokers' circulars to check the companies in question in more detail, ascertain their competitive advantage, confirm that their outlook statements and newsflow are positive, find out if the directors have been buying or selling shares and check the other key statistics.

British-Borneo Petroleum Syndicate

The company has extensive oil interests in the Gulf of Mexico, generally regarded as one of the safest and best oil plays in the world – both politically and geologically. In December 1995 none of the directors had been buying or selling shares and the outlook statement was reasonably confident. Cash flow of 53.1p was sensational, but offset by heavy capital expenditure to fund major expansion. The PEG, unusual in an oil company, was a very attractive 0.43 and the PER only 10, so all the mandatory requirements were in place.

Now for the highly desirable and bonus factors. Most importantly, EPS growth was accelerating – 9% in 1994, 13% forecast for 1995 and 24% for 1996. The market capitalisation was an attractive £130m and there was a useful dividend yield of 3.46%, just below the market average, but good for the sector. Also the price-to-book value of 1.5 provided some underpinning for the share price. All in all it looked very attractive.

Parity

The December 1995 REFS' company entry for Parity is set out below. It is in the old-style half-page format and exemplifies almost all the points I have been making. Parity had a superb graph, positive relative strength, a moderate PER, a very low PEG, a high growth rate, a high return on capital employed, positive cash balances and excellent cash flow. The interim results were excellent and the chairman's view of the future was confident.

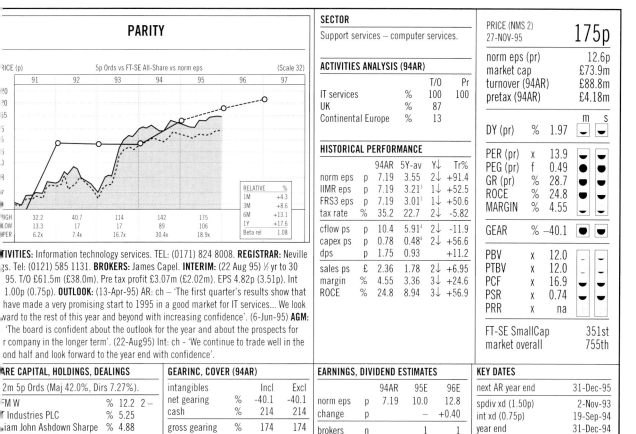

PARITY

PRICE (p) — 5p Ords vs FT-SE All-Share vs norm eps (Scale 32)

	91	92	93	94	95	96	97

RELATIVE %
1M +4.3
3M +8.6
6M +13.1
1Y +17.6
Beta rel 1.08

HIGH	32.2	40.7	114	142	175
LOW	13.3	17	17	89	106
PER	6.2x	7.4x	16.7x	30.4x	18.9x

ACTIVITIES: Information technology services. TEL: (0171) 824 8008. **REGISTRAR:** Neville ... gs. Tel: (0121) 585 1131. **BROKERS:** James Capel. **INTERIM:** (22 Aug 95) ½ yr to 30 ... 95. T/O £61.5m (£38.0m). Pre tax profit £3.07m (£2.02m). EPS 4.82p (3.51p). Int ... 1.00p (0.75p). **OUTLOOK:** (13-Apr-95) AR: ch – 'The first quarter's results show that ... have made a very promising start to 1995 in a good market for IT services... We look ... ward to the rest of this year and beyond with increasing confidence'. (6-Jun-95) **AGM:** ... 'The board is confident about the outlook for the year and about the prospects for ... r company in the longer term'. (22-Aug95) Int: ch - 'We continue to trade well in the ... ond half and look forward to the year end with confidence'.

SECTOR
Support services – computer services.

ACTIVITIES ANALYSIS (94AR)

		T/O	Pr
IT services	%	100	100
UK	%	87	
Continental Europe	%	13	

HISTORICAL PERFORMANCE

		94AR	5Y-av	Y↓	Tr%
norm eps	p	7.19	3.55	2↓	+91.4
IIMR eps	p	7.19	3.21[3]	1↓	+52.5
FRS3 eps	p	7.19	3.01[3]	1↓	+50.6
tax rate	%	35.2	22.7	2↓	-5.82
cflow ps	p	10.4	5.91[4]	2↓	-11.9
capex ps	p	0.78	0.48[4]	2↓	+56.6
dps	p	1.75	0.93		+11.2
sales ps	£	2.36	1.78	2↓	+6.95
margin	%	4.55	3.36	3↓	+24.6
ROCE	%	24.8	8.94	3↓	+56.9

PRICE (NMS 2)
27-NOV-95 — **175p**

norm eps (pr)		12.6p
market cap		£73.9m
turnover (94AR)		£88.8m
pretax (94AR)		£4.18m

			m	s
DY (pr)	%	1.97		

PER (pr)	x	13.9	
PEG (pr)	f	0.49	
GR (pr)	%	28.7	
ROCE	%	24.8	
MARGIN	%	4.55	
GEAR	%	-40.1	
PBV	x	12.0	
PTBV	x	12.0	
PCF	x	16.9	
PSR	x	0.74	
PRR	x	na	

FT-SE SmallCap — 351st
market overall — 755th

ARE CAPITAL, HOLDINGS, DEALINGS

2m 5p Ords (Maj 42.0%, Dirs 7.27%).

FM W	%	12.2	2 –
...T Industries PLC	%	5.25	
...iam John Ashdown Sharpe	%	4.88	
...nuel Montagu & Co Ltd	%	4.74	4 –
...ed Colloids Pension Fund	%	4.17	
...raco Nominees Ltd	%	4.12	
...Swinstead OBE (dch & ce)	%	7.24	
...arbutt* (ch)	k	14.3	
...Thomas Stonor KCB*	k	2.00	

GEARINC, COVER (94AR)

		Incl	Excl
intangibles			
net gearing	%	-40.1	-40.1
cash	%	214	214
gross gearing	%	174	174
under 5 yrs	%	174	174
under 1 yr	%	174	174
quick ratio	r		1.25
current ratio	r		1.25
interest cover	x		8.59
dividend cover	x		4.11

EARNINGS, DIVIDEND ESTIMATES

		94AR	95E	96E
norm eps	p	7.19	10.0	12.8
change	p		–	+0.40
brokers	n		1	1
std dev	p		–	–
growth	%	93.0	39.1	28.0
per	x	24.3	17.5	13.7
dps	p	1.75	2.30	2.80
div yield	%	1.25	1.64	2.00

KEY DATES

next AR year end	31-Dec-95
spdiv xd (1.50p)	2-Nov-93
int xd (0.75p)	19-Sep-94
year end	31-Dec-94
prelim results	7-Mar-95
annual report	13-Apr-95
fin xd (1.00p)	9-May-95
agm	6-Jun-95
int results	22-Aug-95
int xd (1.00p)	25-Sep-95

Parity is involved in the computer consultancy business. The company provides skilled personnel and training to computer users, including two-thirds of the FT-SE 100 companies. It has more than 75,000 freelance systems personnel on its books and vets the quality of their work regularly.

The PSR was an attractive 0.74, but margins were low at only 4.55%. This is because they are based on a fixed percentage of their consultants' remuneration, with Parity acting as the middleman. This is a very difficult business to enter without massive teething problems, so Parity appears to have established for itself a niche in a fast-growing market in an excellent sector. To me the shares seemed to offer a one-way ticket.

Laura Ashley

Although this company passed through the sieves, I would not have bought it in December 1995 because the prospective PER of 34 was far too rich. The growth rate of 69.7% was very high too, but it contained a large element of recovery and benefits from reorganisation, so it could not be sustained for long.

In the event, this decision turned out to be a real howler as by early May 1996 Laura Ashley shares had risen from 130p to 212p. Many investors developing their own systems of share selection may decide not to rule out stocks with very high PERs or to have a higher PEG cut-off. It is very much a question of developing your own investment style. I do not feel comfortable with shares with astronomic PERs in my portfolio, so I usually eliminate them during my sieving process. I realise that by doing so I occasionally miss a stunning investment opportunity but I feel more relaxed sticking to my strict criteria.

Business Post Group

The cluster of black moons in the growth statistics of the December 1995 REFS company entry shows that Business Post combined many attractive characteristics. The PER of 17.4 was on the high side, compared with both the market and the sector. However, the forecast growth rate of 32.1% was near the top of the class and this resulted in a very attractive PEG of 0.54.

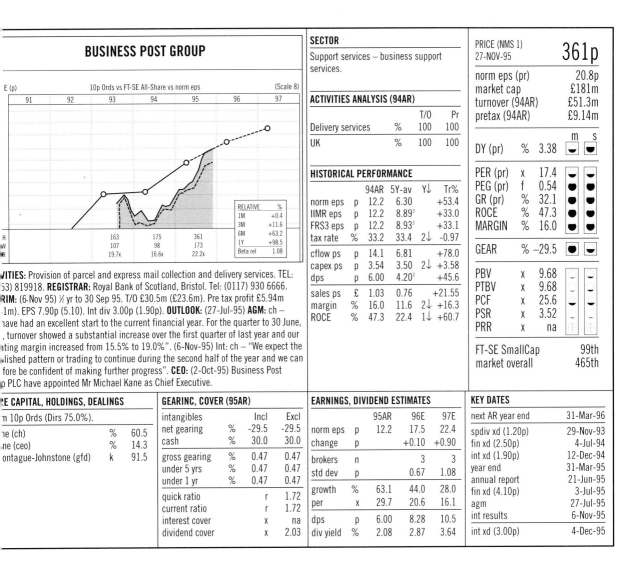

BUSINESS POST GROUP

E (p)   10p Ords vs FT-SE All-Share vs norm eps   (Scale 8)

| 91 | 92 | 93 | 94 | 95 | 96 | 97 |

RELATIVE	%
1M	+0.4
3M	+11.6
6M	+63.2
1Y	+98.5
Beta rel	1.08

H   163   175   361
W   107   98   173
R   19.7x   16.6x   22.2x

VITIES: Provision of parcel and express mail collection and delivery services. TEL: 53) 819918. **REGISTRAR:** Royal Bank of Scotland, Bristol. Tel: (0117) 930 6666. **RIM:** (6-Nov 95) ½ yr to 30 Sep 95. T/O £30.5m (£23.6m). Pre tax profit £5.94m 1m). EPS 7.90p (5.10). Int div 3.00p (1.90p). **OUTLOOK:** (27-Jul-95) **AGM:** ch – have had an excellent start to the current financial year. For the quarter to 30 June, , turnover showed a substantial increase over the first quarter of last year and our ating margin increased from 15.5% to 19.0%". (6-Nov-95) Int: ch – "We expect the lished pattern or trading to continue during the second half of the year and we can fore be confident of making further progress". **CEO:** (2-Oct-95) Business Post p PLC have appointed Mr Michael Kane as Chief Executive.

SECTOR
Support services – business support services.

ACTIVITIES ANALYSIS (94AR)

		T/O	Pr
Delivery services	%	100	100
UK	%	100	100

HISTORICAL PERFORMANCE

		94AR	5Y-av	Y↓	Tr%
norm eps	p	12.2	6.30		+53.4
IIMR eps	p	12.2	8.89[3]		+33.0
FRS3 eps	p	12.2	8.93[3]		+33.1
tax rate	%	33.2	33.4	2↓	-0.97
cflow ps	p	14.1	6.81		+78.0
capex ps	p	3.54	3.50	2↓	+3.58
dps	p	6.00	4.20[3]		+45.6
sales ps	£	1.03	0.76		+21.55
margin	%	16.0	11.6	2↓	+16.3
ROCE	%	47.3	22.4	1↓	+60.7

PRICE (NMS 1)
27-NOV-95   **361p**

norm eps (pr)		20.8p
market cap		£181m
turnover (94AR)		£51.3m
pretax (94AR)		£9.14m

			m	s
DY (pr)	%	3.38		
PER (pr)	x	17.4		
PEG (pr)	f	0.54		
GR (pr)	%	32.1		
ROCE	%	47.3		
MARGIN	%	16.0		
GEAR	%	-29.5		
PBV	x	9.68		
PTBV	x	9.68		
PCF	x	25.6		
PSR	x	3.52		
PRR	x	na		

FT-SE SmallCap   99th
market overall   465th

E CAPITAL, HOLDINGS, DEALINGS
m 10p Ords (Dirs 75.0%).

ne (ch)	%	60.5
ne (ceo)	%	14.3
ontague-Johnstone (gfd)	k	91.5

GEARINC, COVER (95AR)

		Incl	Excl
intangibles			
net gearing	%	-29.5	-29.5
cash	%	30.0	30.0
gross gearing	%	0.47	0.47
under 5 yrs	%	0.47	0.47
under 1 yr	%	0.47	0.47
quick ratio	r		1.72
current ratio	r		1.72
interest cover	x		na
dividend cover	x		2.03

EARNINGS, DIVIDEND ESTIMATES

		95AR	96E	97E
norm eps	p	12.2	17.5	22.4
change	p		+0.10	+0.90
brokers	n		3	3
std dev	p		0.67	1.08
growth	%	63.1	44.0	28.0
per	x	29.7	20.6	16.1
dps	p	6.00	8.28	10.5
div yield	%	2.08	2.87	3.64

KEY DATES

next AR year end	31-Mar-96
spdiv xd (1.20p)	29-Nov-93
fin xd (2.50p)	4-Jul-94
int xd (1.90p)	12-Dec-94
year end	31-Mar-95
annual report	21-Jun-95
fin xd (4.10p)	3-Jul-95
agm	27-Jul-95
int results	6-Nov-95
int xd (3.00p)	4-Dec-95

Cash flow of 14.1p was healthily above EPS of 12.2p for 1995 and, on the five-year average, 6.8p was just above 6.3p. Capex of 3.5p for 1995 was also well covered by cash flow of 14.1p. EPS growth was slowing down after averaging 53.4% during the previous five years, but the forecast rate of 32.1% seemed to be reasonably sustainable. ROCE was terrific at 47.3% and, according to the chairman, margins had increased again recently to 19%. As a consequence, the PSR was on the high side at 3.52.

Business Post is about the tenth largest parcels and express mail organisation in the UK with a market share of 4%. The company was growing fast and the outlook statement was very positive. A reciprocal link had recently been forged in Europe, which was seen as a major source of future business. The competitive advantage of Business Post rests in its reputation for reliability and the very broad range of services it offers. The company obtained BS5750 accreditation in 1994 and its exceptional growth record and growing margins vouch for its efficiency. In December 1995 it had a network of 16 regional hubs, a national hub in Birmingham and 45 franchised local depots. Although there is plenty of competition, it would be difficult for a newcomer to start from scratch. The shares seemed to me to be a strong buy.

Rutland Trust

This company was very hard to define as, under the management of Michael Langdon, its shape had changed substantially and seemingly very much for the better.

The prospective PER of 13.6 was about average but the growth rate of 23.3% was well above the norm, resulting in an inviting PEG of 0.58. EPS for 1994 of only 2.3p was massively exceeded by cash flow per share of 11.6p giving, at 40p, a very low PCF of only 3.44. The future outlook seemed bright from the chairman's interim statement, especially as the interim dividend was increased by 10%.

The problem was gearing of 236%, mainly caused by Rutland buying Thamesport during 1995. To help fund the purchase it sold off Leasecontracts, one of its most profitable subsidiaries. Thamesport can be substantially expanded and, as a port, possesses a strong competitive advantage. It also brought with it extremely useful tax losses of £60m plus a further £60m of capital allowances. The deal seemed to me to be a brilliant one and I much admired the courage of Michael Langdon and the board in making such a sweeping change. It would not take long for gearing to be reduced to more normal levels, as exceptionally strong cash flow helped by a much reduced tax charge began to eat into it. By my calculations gearing would be reduced to below 75% before the end of 1996. Rutland Trust therefore had my vote as a strong buy and was an excellent example of the kind of compromises that are often made when making final selections.

In this context, it is interesting to note that I included Independent Insurance in my New Year portfolio for the *Financial Mail on Sunday*, although it was rejected in our early analysis for this portfolio on the grounds of poor relative strength for the month and three months.

During December, the shares forged ahead and quickly became a buy on my criteria as relative strength for the previous 12 months turned positive.

I double-checked Independent Insurance with two relatives who happen to be insurance brokers. Both had a very high opinion of the company and one of them had already purchased some shares for his portfolio. It was included in my *Financial Mail* portfolio at 375p and by June 1996 the shares had risen to 461p, after flirting with 500p in April and May.

The examples of Rutland Trust and Independent Insurance illustrated an important principle. REFS is an invaluable sieve for highlighting the shares with the lowest PEGs in each index at the end of every month. It also shows, in the accompanying columns, cash flow in relation to EPS and relative strength for the previous year and previous month. However, the company entry, the annual report, profiles in *Analyst*, reviews in the *Investors Chronicle* and in newsletters and brokers' circulars help to flesh out the pure arithmetic.

REFS' evidence to date indicates that you would beat the market by simply taking the top shares in the tables and applying the sieves without using any further supplementary information. However, I believe that you should fare even better if you learn to compromise when necessary. The confidence to do this will come gradually.

It is important to monitor your success or failure in departing from a strictly arithmetical approach. It would therefore be worthwhile to record carefully any departures from sticking to the basic formulae. The results of your initiatives can then be evaluated and compared. If over a period they do not pay off, there is a simple remedy.

As you can see, by the end of May 1996, the four shares in the portfolio had appreciated in price substantially:

	Price 27.11.95 p	Price 29.5.96 p	Gain %
British-Borneo Petroleum	242*	594.0	145.5
Parity	175	280.0	60.0
Business Post Group	361	439.0	21.6
Rutland Trust	40	52.5	31.2
AVERAGE GAIN			64.6

* The purchase price of British-Borneo Petroleum has been reduced to allow for the sale of rights to two shares for every five. On the last day of trading the nil paid rights could have been sold for 119p. This reduced the purchase price by 47.6p.

During the six months the market measured by the FT-SE All-Share index rose by only 5.84% and the more appropriate measure, the FT-SE SmallCap index, rose by 14.2%. British-Borneo was, of course, the best performer by a very wide margin but, in any portfolio, there is usually one star and investment is essentially a business of averages. It is pleasing to note that every share in the portfolio beat the SmallCap index substantially and the average performance was about 4.5 times that of the index and 11 times the market's miserable 5.84%. Costs have been ignored but these would have been relatively trivial and would have hardly affected the overall results.

In the above analysis we only worked from the FT-SE SmallCap index. In the same December 1995 issue of REFS there were some very inviting shares in the Fledgling index. There were also a large number in the table of non-index companies, which is usually full at the end of the year, before the Review Panel promotes most of the shares to an index, usually the Fledgling.

In particular, in the non-index table, JJB Sports at 510p (June 96 – 818p) was at the top with a PEG of 0.32, Photobition was second at 320p (June 96 – 370p) on a PEG of 0.39 and Oasis Stores at 222p (June 96 – 404p) was a little lower down with a PEG of 0.75. I held all of them in my portfolio.

In the Fledgling index I held shares in Azlan Group at 495p (June 96 – 665p) with a PEG of only 0.47, Groupe Chez Gerard at 198p (June 96 – 255p) with a PEG of 0.65, and Pressac at 142p (June 96 – 177p) with a PEG of 0.75 and extremely high cash flow.

Forte, at 347p, was still at the top of the FT-SE 100 index with a PEG of 0.78, even after the Granada bid. Bank of Scotland, GKN, Asda Group, Nat West, Rentokil and British Airways all had PEGs of under 1.0. Interestingly, Forte had been at the top of the October tables too, when the price was only 248p and the PEG only 0.52. (Maybe fewer institutions were subscribing to REFS in those days).

Shares with low PEGs are always quite well represented in the Mid-250 Index. IMI at 312p (June 96 – 361p) was at the top with a PEG of 0.30 and Lucas was second at 185p (June 96 – 241p on bid rumours) with a PEG of 0.53. In the top 15, an old favourite of mine, Carpetright at 394p (June 96 – 613p) had a PEG of 0.69, Stagecoach Holdings at 279p (June 96 – 444p) had a PEG of 0.72, BBA at 284p (June 96 – 328p) had a PEG of 0.67 and Matthew Clark at 647p (June 96 – 801p) had a PEG of 0.66.

I have shown the closing prices on 3 June 1996 in brackets in each case to highlight the attractiveness of the shares featured in the low PEG tables *only six months earlier*. There are usually plenty of shares with interesting PEGs in every monthly issue of REFS. The more marketable the shares in the index, the higher the average PEG. In the FT-SE 100 index, there were only eight shares with PEGs below 1.0, in the Mid-250 there were 28 and in the prolific FT-SE SmallCap a whole page of 55 companies ended on a cut-off of 0.85. There were only 40 companies with PEGs of under 1.0 in the Fledgling, for the reasons I have already explained.

There were 18 companies with PEGs of under 1.0 in the table of non-index companies, which has proved to be another very attractive hunting ground for cheap stocks. Quite often new issues take a few months to find their proper level in the market.

The buying of shares is, of course, of vital importance, but the question I am most often asked at conferences is when they should be sold. The answer is complex, involving capital gains tax and other general portfolio management considerations, all of which will be covered in the next chapter.

SUMMARY

1. My suggested criteria for selecting growth shares to beat the market are as follows:

    a) *Mandatory*

        1. A PEG with a relatively low cut-off such as 0.75.

        2. A prospective PER of not more than 20. The preferred range for PERs is 10–20 with forecast growth rates of 15–30%.

        3. Strong cash flow per share in excess of EPS, both for the last reported year and for the five-year average.

        4. Positive cash or gearing of below 50%, other than in exceptional circumstances (such as really massive cash flow per share or impending sales of major assets).

        5. High relative strength for the previous twelve months.

        6. A competitive advantage, which will usually be evidenced by a high ROCE and good operating margins.

        7. No selling of shares by a cluster of directors.

    b) *Highly desirable*

        1. Accelerating EPS, especially if it is a result of activities being cloned.

        2. A cluster of directors buying shares.

        3. A small market capitalisation in the £30m–250m range.

        4. A dividend yield.

    c) *Bonus*

        1. A low PSR.

2. Something new.

3. A low PRR.

4. A reasonable asset position.

Very few shares will satisfy all of the mandatory and highly desirable criteria. A share may meet almost all of the criteria very strongly indeed, but just fall short on one of them. In these kinds of instances, it is necessary to compromise a little.

15

PORTFOLIO MANAGEMENT

In the previous chapter, I mentioned the New Year's portfolio I recommended to readers of the *Financial Mail on Sunday*. I tried to put the shares in order of attractiveness, but I warned readers that '...this is always difficult as some may surprise us'. Here is the portfolio based on buying prices on the preceding Friday, which was the last day of trading in 1995:

NEW YEAR PORTFOLIO							
	Buying Price p	Prospective PER	EPS growth rate %	PEG	Cashflow/ EPS ratio	One year relative strength %	One month relative strength %
Business Post	378	17.1	30	0.58	1.2	+85	+1.9
JJB Sports	575	17.3	29	0.60	1.1	+113	+11.3
Grosvenor Inns	250	17.2	37	0.46	1.9	+51	+1.2
Parity	177	13.7	28	0.49	1.4	+18	−0.8
More O'Ferrall	459	14.0	21	0.67	1.4	+6	+0.1
Pressac	148	12.8	17	0.74	2.3	+30	+2.0
Pelican Group	125	13.9	34	0.41	1.6	+25	+6.4
Ind. Ins. Group	375	7.0	10	0.67	n.a.	+19	+8.5

And here are the results for the six months ended 30 June 1996 based on selling prices on the last day of trading:

	Buying Price 29.12.95	Selling Price 28.6.95	Profit	Gain
	p	p	p	%
Business Post	378	438	60	15.9
JJB Sports	192*	260	68	35.4
Grosvenor Inns	250	262	12	4.8
Parity	177	260	83	46.9
More O'Ferrall	459	650	191	41.6
Pressac	148	193	45	30.4
Pelican Group	125	152	27	21.6
Ind. Ins. Group	375	461	86	22.9
AVERAGE GAIN				27.4

*Buying price adjusted for 2 for 1 bonus issue in June 1996.

Dividends were ignored and the selling prices used were the lowest that could have been obtained. The closing price of Business Post, for example, was 438–445p; there was modest demand for the shares on Friday 28 June, so instead of 438p it would probably have been possible to sell at 439p or 440p. Brokers' commissions and stamp duty would have cost about another 1.5% in total and the price of the eight shares rose the day after my recommendations by an average of 3.5%. Therefore, net of all costs and after allowing for the effect of press comment, the final profit would have been 22.4%. During the six-month period, the FT-SE Actuaries All-Share index rose by only 3.0% and the FT-SE SmallCap by 12.4%, in spite of being flattered in the usual way by using middle-market to middle-market prices and by excluding dealing costs. In this case, the All-Share was the more appropriate index to measure performance against as the eight shares were found by sieving the whole market.

There are some lessons to be learned from the performance of this portfolio:

1. The individual order of attractiveness of shares is difficult to judge and of no real importance. Investment is essentially a business of averages and quite often of surprises.

2. It is important to spread risk over a number of shares. If all my eggs had been in the basket of my top choice, Business Post, the results would have been comparatively disappointing. Indeed, by April, the Business Post share price had hardly risen and the shares only got into their stride in May.

    Although you know with low PEG stocks that a status change is very likely to happen, you never know *when* the shares will take off. However keen you are on a particular share, never bet the bank.

3. The margin of safety provided by low PEGs was illustrated by Grosvenor Inns. The interim results announced in February 1996 were disappointing. Growth in EPS had slackened from a forecast 47% to about 25%. However, the share price only fell a little, before quickly recovering, as 25% was still a very substantial and well above average rate of growth in relation to the undemanding PER at the time of purchase.

4. The average anticipated EPS annual growth rate of the eight selections was 25.75%. Over six months, EPS growth could therefore be argued to account for 12.87% of the rise in share prices. The balance came from status changes in the PERs. This double whammy effect is the main benefit of buying shares with low PEGs.

5. An added attraction of buying shares with low PEGs is that even after a significant rise they often still appear to be cheap. JJB Sports, Business Post and Parity, for example, were still on PEGs of under 0.8 and five directors of Independent Insurance bought more shares in March 1996 at over 460p.

HOW MANY SHARES?

In a letter written to a friend in 1934, John Maynard Keynes concluded after many years of successful investing: 'As time goes on, I get more and more convinced that the right method of investment is to put fairly large sums into enterprises which one thinks one knows something about and in the management of which one thoroughly believes. It is a mistake to think one limits one's risk by spreading too much between enterprises about which one knows little and has no reason for special confidence.'

Warren Buffett also believes that concentrating upon a few shares may well decrease risk, if it raises the intensity with which investors think about a business and the level of comfort they need to feel before buying into the share in question. It is a mystery to Buffett why investors elect to put money into their twentieth choice rather than adding to their top choice. With the now massive funds under his control, he continues to practise what he preaches.

It is, of course, all very well for investors of the calibre of Keynes and Buffett to advise concentrating a portfolio on just a few stocks. Almost all of the time, they would know exactly what they were doing and they would be capable of thoroughly analysing a stock and obtaining the necessary level of confidence before committing a relatively large part of their portfolio to it. Most investors are aware that they do not have the ability of Keynes and Buffett and therefore, quite rightly, lack their confidence.

I suggest that ten to twelve shares is about the right number for the portfolio of a private investor with up to about £50,000 to invest. For £500,000, about fifteen shares would be more appropriate and for £1m up to twenty or perhaps a little more. This does not mean that with a portfolio of, say, twelve shares exactly 8.5% of the total fund should be invested in each share. The percentages should be weighted towards those shares which provide the investor with the highest degree of comfort. Perhaps an outstanding favourite share would merit 12.5–15% of the money to be invested. About 8.5% might then be invested in a few of the shares and the balance of the portfolio could contain some comparatively negligible shareholdings. Quite often I find that I decide to buy a share and can only obtain a few before it bounds ahead. When this happens I usually keep the holding for a while in the hope that the shares will come back to allow me to buy some more. If, however, they go on rising, I usually decide to sell, as I do not like my portfolio to be cluttered with too many small and irrelevant holdings.

All of the above ideas are, of course, based on allocating percentages of a portfolio on a *cost* basis. In practice, this soon becomes irrelevant. Based on market value, a really successful investment can quickly become 20–25% of a portfolio and this brings us to the most difficult question of all – when to sell?

WARREN BUFFETT'S APPROACH TO SELLING

Warren Buffett is credited with being the kind of investor who ignores the market and likes to hold shares for ever. Investors studying his very successful methods should distinguish between his company's core holdings (quasi-partnerships) and more general investments. Of course, if a company is doing well and its shares are going from strength to strength, it pays to run the profits. *The oldest and best axiom in investment is to run profits and cut losses – that way profits are likely to be large and losses are bound to be small.*

In the 1987 report of Berkshire Hathaway, Warren Buffett spells out his approach to selling marketable investments. He first makes it clear that he judges his holdings not by their market prices, but their operating results. As Benjamin Graham said, 'In the short run, the market is a voting machine, but in the long run, it is a weighing machine.' His point was that eventually the market will recognise superior operating results (and increased value) but he did not worry unduly if this took a few years to happen. Buffett is completely confident of his ability to judge the value of a company and confident that, in the end, the market will recognise that he is right. He goes on to explain that his monitoring of operating results is to ensure that 'The company's intrinsic value is increasing at a satisfactory rate.' The implication is that if this is not the case he sells, as indeed he did with his company's first British investment, Guinness.

Warren Buffett draws attention to two other reasons that would prompt him to make a sale:

1. When the market judges a company to be more valuable than the underlying facts would indicate. (The only exception is a core quasi-partnership holding.)

2. When funds are required to invest in a security that is 'still more under-valued'.

Buffett further qualifies his approach by saying that he does not sell holdings simply because they have risen in price or because they have been held for a long time. He scorns the Wall Street axiom 'You can't go broke taking a profit' and is happy to remain a holder indefinitely *provided* the return on capital is satisfactory, management is both competent and honest and the market does not overvalue the business. As you can see, these are heavy provisos.

Another reason put forward by Buffett for holding on to exceptional growth shares with competent and honest management is that they are very hard to find and that dealing in shares costs money as well as sometimes crystallising a capital gains tax liability. When a share, that is not held in a PEP or personal pension plan, has had a really good run in the market, the potential capital gains tax liability can be many times the original cost. Provided you continue to hold the shares, the Government, in effect, makes you an interest-free loan of the tax that will eventually have to be paid. This loan helps to increase very substantially the capital appreciation on the investment as there are no interest charges and your investment is geared without the usual worry of how the loan will be repaid.

HAS THE STORY CHANGED?

In *The Zulu Principle*, I suggested that the main reason to sell a share was if the story had changed. By this I meant any change in the key factors that had attracted you to the shares in the first place. If, for example, the company's profits were faltering, a major new competitor had entered the arena and begun a price war, or the company had lost a major source of business, the shares should be sold immediately.

In normal market conditions, with an exceptional growth share that is continuing to do its thing and produce excellent year on year results, it pays to retain your holding even if the PEG rises to a slightly uncomfortable level. A PEG of 1.2 (in relation to a market average of 1.5) is as high as I would personally allow, as the margin of safety would have shrunk to a level that would make me feel ill at ease. However, I could well understand some investors deciding to hold on to their favourite investment, even if the PEG rose to the market average. Above that, I would recommend selling and bidding a reluctant *au revoir* to the shares. If you keep an eye on them, there will almost certainly be another opportunity to buy at a much more favourable price. Meanwhile, your money can be better used in a share that is due for an upward status change, not a downward one.

RELATIVE STRENGTH

The most difficult problem arises when a share suddenly begins to perform badly in the market for no apparent reason. After a substantial rise, great growth shares often encounter profit-taking so, from one month to another, their relative strength might be poor. If the trend persists and they show poor relative strength over the previous three months, that is definitely a cause for concern.

If one of your shares performs badly for several weeks, you should ask your broker for an explanation. There may be a market story that accounts for the poor performance. For example, a key executive might be planning to leave the company, there could be news of an impending major lawsuit or of fresh competition entering the market. The other obvious source for this kind of information is press cuttings and a final option is to telephone the company and ask one of the directors or the company secretary if he or she knows of any reason for the shares' poor relative performance.

If you can find an explanation, the key question then is whether or not the underlying story (what persuaded you to buy the shares in the first place) has changed. Re-examine the share, in light of all the available facts, including the current brokers' consensus forecast, and ask yourself if you would still buy the shares today. If the answer is yes, grit your teeth and hold on.

Some people believe in averaging, which means buying shares on (hopefully) short-term weakness to reduce the average cost of their investment. I recommend you to resist this temptation. I prefer to buy more of a share that is rising – reinforcing success seems to me to be a better approach than compounding failure.

STOP LOSS

Some investors will find that they cannot stand the worry of a share continuing to fall, particularly when no explanation can be found. Many commentators recommend stop-loss systems and if this is going to make you sleep better, by all means use one. You can, for example, set a stop-loss at 20% below your purchase price or a trailing stop-loss of, say, 20–25% below the highest price registered by the shares. The trailing stop-loss means that if the share does very well in the early stages, you make sure of locking in some profit.

My preference is to hang in there, until I can find the reason for the fall. A low PEG provides a margin of safety and buying shares in a systematic way is very different from speculating in, for example, bio-tech and concept stocks, which often have no earnings and no commercial products. With these kinds of shares a trailing stop-loss is mandatory. I do not recommend buying them though – why gamble when you have a formula that works?

PEPS

PEPs should be used to the maximum possible extent. The 1996 allowance for each individual is £6,000 for a general PEP and £3,000 for a single company PEP.

Some sizeable private investors may feel that PEPs are not worth the trouble as to them the annual allowances appear to be derisory. They are not taking into account the cumulative effect of the tax-free growth PEPs offer investors. Over the years the annual allowances, together with capital gains, can accumulate to a very sizeable tax-free pool of money – a kind of tax haven in your own back yard.

Shares held in PEPs form an integral part of an overall portfolio but, as they operate tax-free, the arguments for running profits in them are less acute. The general principle of running profits does, of course, continue to apply, but the pregnant tax liability is no longer a consideration.

Near to the end of the tax year, it clearly pays to review your portfolio and absorb your permitted annual tax-exempt capital gains allowance (£6,000 in 1996), even if this is simply achieved by bed-and-breakfasting some of your shares.

FILES

I recommend keeping a file on each investment. It should contain the last couple of annual and interim reports, copies of any other announcements, press cuttings and any brokers' circulars that you have managed to obtain. It is also a useful reminder to set out in writing, in a few words, exactly why you invested in the company in the first place. To remind you of the exact circumstances, it may also help to add to the file a photocopy of the REFS company entry at the time.

In addition to company files, it is advisable to record investments in an investment ledger. When noting the prices of any shares purchased, also make a note of the level of the FT-SE Actuaries All-Share index on the day of the transaction. This will give you a useful measure against which to gauge the performance of individual shares and of your portfolio as a whole. If you can spare the time, try to compare performance once a week, if not once a fortnight or, at the very least, once a month.

SUMMARY

1. The portfolio of most private investors should contain about 10–15 shares, rising to about 30 for a sizeable fund.

2. Do not bet the bank on one share. Up to 15% is about the right maximum investment based on cost.

3. Use PEPs to the fullest possible extent and ensure that you absorb your annual capital gains tax allowance (£6,000 in 1996) every year, even if you simply do this by bed-and-breakfasting.

4. Run profits and cut losses.

5. Sell shares when the story has changed (e.g. the company's intrinsic value is no longer increasing at the required rate), the market awards the company too high a PEG (say 80% of the market average) or funds are required for a better, more undervalued investment. Bear in mind that a very substantial pregnant capital gains tax liability can make it advisable to stretch the PEG selling limit to the market average, but not beyond it.

6. Record investments in a ledger and regularly measure performance against the FT-SE Actuaries All-Share index. If, over a period of say three or more years, you find that you are not beating the market, you should consider delegating the management of your portfolio to a professional fund manager via unit trusts or the like.

16

BULL AND BEAR MARKETS

Investors who buy shares for the long term and insist on a margin of safety (such as a low PEG) at the time of purchase, have little to fear from the vagaries of the market. When the bear is rampant, share prices will be savaged, but as long as the companies in question continue to grow, and their EPS continue to increase, the market will eventually reflect the progress they have been making.

The first key point is to invest only 'patient money' that can be locked up and will not be needed suddenly. The second is to buy systematically with a margin of safety and to hold long term. Warren Buffett advises investors to pretend that they have been issued with a punch-card with a space for 20 holes. As they make each investment, a hole is punched in the card. After 20 investments, the card would be full of holes and there would be no more investing for life. The essence of Buffett's message is that the greatest care should be taken in selecting shares. It is not a casual experience that should be undertaken lightly.

There is no doubt that, at times, one feels far more bullish than at others. For example, the Coppock Indicator is usually a reliable buy signal. On the day it suggests that the market should be bought, I would be happy to be 100% invested, possibly even more. At other times, when the Coppock Indicator has run its average course of about 14 months and there is far too much confidence and complacency in the air, I would prefer to be more liquid. However, active investors usually have at least 75% of their patient money invested in the market. Everyone's temperament is different so, in a bearish climate, some investors may prefer to tune this down perhaps to 50%. If investments are keeping you awake at night, it is obviously important to reduce the percentage invested down to your sleep level. This procedure will also be far more effective if shares with the highest PEGs and those that you are least certain about are sold first. As a result, the average PEG of your residual portfolio will be reduced to a lower and more attractive level with a greater margin of safety.

It is important to realise that bull markets climb a wall of worry and, as Joe Granville puts it, 'Bear markets never visit by appointment ringing your front doorbell by daylight, they come like a thief in the night.' It can therefore be argued that the more worried most investors feel, the more likely it is that shares are about to go up. The logic behind this is, of course, that if most investors are very worried, they will have sold already and many professionals will be short. The slightest glimmer of good news would then be sufficient to cause a buying panic.

Crowd psychology is explained in Gustave le Bon's classic book *The Crowd* and in Charles Mackay's excellent book *Extraordinary Popular Delusions and the Madness of Crowds*. The driving forces are fear and greed and it is important to understand that manias are not a thing of the past – they are always developing and are very much a feature of markets today. The mania for Japanese stocks in the eighties and the current mania for technology stocks are good examples. You can see how easily they develop – someone at a golf club might mention to another member how much money he had made on technology stocks. A friend mentions at a dinner party the superb performance of a technology trust. There are plenty of enthusiastic articles on technology stocks in the newspapers and then a broker recommends a new technology issue. The investor succumbs and does well and is soon looking for another similar opportunity. Prices rise from general buying pressure and, as they do, the extra performance generated feeds the greed of eager buyers. The mania continues until there are a few failures and major disappointments. Then a few people start pointing at technology stocks and saying that the king has no clothes. As technology shares begin to fall, investors panic and rush for the exit. The downward spiral causes a panic and shares fall further until they reach bargain-basement levels. After a period of consolidation, they then become ready for the next boom.

SIGNS OF A BEAR MARKET

There are a number of signs that may help you to detect when the market is in a bull or bear phase. However, formulae do not always work. The bear is wily and appears each time in a different form. There are usually subtle variations distinguishing each bear market from previous ones but, subject to this proviso, here are some major pointers that might help to warn you when one is on the way:

1. Cash is usually regarded as a very undesirable asset. As a result, the cash balances of institutional and private investors will usually be at very low levels. American fund managers describe the mood well: 'Cash is trash.'

2. Value will be hard to find. The average PEG will be 1.5 or more and there will be few, if any, stocks at a substantial discount to asset values.

3. The average dividend yield will be at historically very low levels.

4. Interest rates will usually be about to rise. Certainly the chances of them falling further will be minimal.

5. The consensus of investment advisers will be bullish and the general mood of investors will be upbeat.

6. New issues will be rampant and of increasingly low quality. The fundamentals of each issue will be less relevant to investors than how many shares they can get hold of to make a quick turn and be ready to subscribe for the next one.

7. The ratio of directors buying to directors selling will have fallen to historically low levels.

8. Shares will be failing to respond to good results – even those of companies that beat their forecasts. This is a sign of the market's exhaustion and that very little buying power remains.

9. The market will be the subject on everyone's lips at cocktail and dinner parties. Enthusiasm for shares and unit trusts will also be evidenced by the increased space given to investment by newspapers and magazines. (It was, therefore, worrying to hear that in July 1996 *Reader's Digest* had a cover story proclaiming that striking it rich in the stock market 'is within anyone's grasp.')

10. When over 75% of all the stocks in the market have been standing above their long-term averages, if the number of stocks then falls below 75% that is usually a bearish technical signal.

11. On average, about 14 months will have elapsed since the last Coppock Indicator buying signal, during which time the average gain (based on the last ten buying signals) would have been about 30%. However, on one occasion, the gain was only 8%, so do not rely too much on the average expectation.

12. Broad money supply will usually be contracting.

13. A major change in market leadership will take place. Cyclicals usually do well near the top of bull markets.

All of the above points work in reverse for deciding whether or not it is time to buy at the bottom of a bear market. For example, it is usually recognised then that cash is without question the best possible asset to own. Cash is no longer trash, it will have become king.

CHARACTERISTICS OF BULL AND BEAR MARKETS

There are a number of points to be made about bull and bear markets:

1. Bull markets last much longer than bear markets, but a great deal of money can be lost in a very short time in a vicious bear market. For example, in 1973–5, 75% was wiped off UK market values.

2. There is no real difference between a major correction in a bull market and a mini-bear market. A technical purist would argue that after the 1987 crash the market recovered and went above its previous high, suggesting that the bull market was still intact, and 1987 was simply a major correction.
   A major bear market is different – a prolonged period of at least nine months and sometimes as much as two to three years, during which bearish conditions prevail and investors wish they were somewhere else.

3. In the eighties, global markets seemed to move in step. During the days after the 1987 crash, a sharp afternoon fall on Wall Street would have a knock-on effect in Tokyo overnight, which in turn would weaken opening prices in London the next morning. But less than five years later, Japan had more than halved, while both Wall Street and London had reached all-time highs.

In the final analysis, no major country can succeed in isolation. If the world economy falls into a deep recession, there is no doubt that every major stock market will be affected. Nevertheless, there does seem to be more scope today for a number of individual stock markets to rise, even if some of the other major markets in the world are in a down-trend.

4. Both bull and bear markets have several different stages. At the beginning of a bear market, there is usually a sharp fall during which economic conditions remain positive. Subsequently, economic conditions deteriorate but the market becomes over-sold. There is then a sucker's rally, powerful enough to persuade most investors into believing that the market has bottomed. Then, the economic news becomes awful and investors panic and sell at any price. The market declines very sharply as the downward spiral becomes self-feeding. This last stage is only over, and ready as a springboard for the next bull market, when investors abandon all hope for the future. The first positive sign will be that shares no longer fall on bad news.

Any treatise on bear markets makes one feel gloomy and frightened. However, it is important for investors to be frightened periodically, if only to force them to audit their portfolios and cast out any doubtful or speculative shares. This will improve their liquidity and the quality of their portfolios and enable them to ride the storm. When the outlook becomes brighter, their residual well-chosen shares will be among the quickest to rise from the wreckage.

SUMMARY

1. Only invest 'patient money' that will not be needed suddenly.

2. Buy shares systematically *with a margin of safety* and hold for the long term. As explained in Chapter 2, selection is far more important than timing.

3. There are a number of signs that may help you to detect when the market is about to turn downward. These are set out in detail on pages 159–60.

4. If the market outlook appears to be really grim and the percentage of your patient money invested is causing you to lose sleep, reduce it to your sleep level. However, you could easily be wrong as bull markets often climb a wall of worry, so do not reduce your long-term investments below 50% of your patient money.

    When selling shares, choose those with the highest PEGs and the ones that satisfy the fewest of your investment criteria. In this way you will improve your liquidity and lower the average PEG of your portfolio which will, in turn, increase your margin of safety.

5. The Coppock Indicator is one of the most reliable signs of an impending bull market.

17

TECHNOLOGY STOCKS

No book on growth shares would be complete without a chapter on technology. The Americans dub the high-tech sector 'the market that beats the market', reflecting the breathtaking way their technology stocks have outperformed the market as a whole. Since 1990, many stocks have increased in price more than ten-fold and still seem to have plenty of go left in them.

You can readily see why American investors are so enthusiastic about technology stocks and why there is an increasing interest in them in the UK. We have had a few high-flyers too, but the shares of our star performers tend to be much smaller and more illiquid than their American counterparts. Nevertheless, technology is the sector of the future and no growth investor can ignore it.

INTERNET

In early 1996 'Internet' is still the word that most excites investors in technology stocks. Any company that has any connection, however slight, with the Internet is almost certain to enjoy a premium rating in the stock market.

As the Internet is likely to be of such future importance to investors, I invited Conor McCarthy, the editor of *Techinvest*, to define it for me. This is what he had to say in April 1996:

> The Internet is a loosely configured web of around 40,000 corporate, educational and research computer networks around the world. It evolved from an R and D communications network created by the US Department of Defense in 1969 to ensure that a nationwide communications facility would continue to operate in the aftermath of nuclear war.
>
> The network was therefore designed on simple principles. There would be no central control point or authority, as any

nuclear attack would obviously aim to take it out. The route followed by interconnections would be impossible to predict in advance since an attack might have wiped out complete chunks of the network. All nodes in the network would, therefore, be equal in status to all other nodes; each would have its own authority to originate, pass and receive messages.

The messages themselves would be divided into electronically coded packets of 1s and 0s; each packet would be separately addressed, wandering through the network, from node to node, until it found its destination.

The basic design principles prevail on the Internet to this day and are the very reason why it can spread and replicate so effortlessly. A message will get through provided it conforms to the internationally recognised TCP/IP protocol. This is a technical, not a social or political standard, one reason why totalitarian regimes abhor the Internet.

Any standard network that complies with the requirements itself becomes part of the Internet. Up to 1989, commercial services were not supposed to connect to the Internet. Now they are starting to dominate it. As a result, use of the system is growing like wildfire. The current number of users is about 35 million.

In theory, the Internet is controlled by its users. But there is no official Internet which you pay to join. Instead, each group of people accessing the Internet is responsible for their part of it.

Since the Internet is anarchic in nature it is not simple to use. Commercial companies, like Unipalm, have sprung up to facilitate making connections to the Internet. Other companies, such as Netscape in America, have created software that makes it much easier to ramble around the Internet, find what you want, extract it and present it in a user-friendly form.

The Internet is used to exchange data between geographically dispersed locations. This may be either computer data or electronic mail. Remote access is also available to many commercial subscription and public databases. News and information can be exchanged through thousands of electronic bulletin boards and discussion groups, which cover an almost infinite range of topics.

The Internet can be accessed from any home connected to the telephone network; all that is needed is a PC, a modem and a small monthly subscription to a local service provider. After that, all you pay is the cost of a local call, no matter where you connect to in the world or for how long.

As you can see, users of the Internet currently obtain their information for just the cost of a local call. The suppliers of information hope that the 'surfers' who ride the Internet waves will become addicted and, when a charging system is introduced on a time-used basis, they will be prepared to pay for the information they require. This seems to me to be a rather nebulous concept on which to base the massive market capitalisations enjoyed by some technology companies. The present mania would make Benjamin Graham, the father of value investing, turn in his grave.

In spite of the froth, it is difficult not to get caught up in the general enthusiasm for computer stocks. In early July 1996, the Gartner Group, leading IT industry analysts, estimated that the total costs of making the essential modifications for the millennium would be $120bn for Europe alone. (Many computers presently only store and process the last two digits of any year, so unless some changes are made they will not know which century they refer to.)

A few days after the Gartner Group forecast, IBM warned that the computer industry would be in chaos if European monetary union starts as planned in 1999. IBM predicted that there would be an acute shortage of the necessary skills to handle the transition, especially as the date is so near to the computer overhauls needed to cope with the end of the century.

These two major events, coupled with the growing importance of the Internet and the continuing massive advances in technology, should ensure that computer services companies have a wonderfully buoyant time during the next three or four years. With this industrial backcloth, it is hard to imagine a better business to be engaged in than supplying expert computer staff, assisting with training programmes and providing solutions to difficult computer problems, such as viruses and complete changeovers to new systems. Hardware and software suppliers should also benefit from the extraordinarily good trading conditions, but in their case it is more a question of having the right products at the right time.

FIVE MAIN CLASSIFICATIONS

You have probably gathered that I am a keen investor in the technology stocks that appeal to me. However, I like to have my cake and eat it, so I invest in only those shares which also measure up to my financial criteria.

In my view, there are several distinct types of technology stocks, with different approaches needed to evaluate each of them:

1. *LEADING established companies*

    In America, Microsoft and Hewlett Packard are good examples of leading electronics companies. In the UK, mobile phone operator Vodafone, capitalised at over £8bn, Orange and Cellnet part-owner Securicor, both capitalised at over £1bn, are perhaps the nearest equivalents, even though they are not really high-tech. They are, however, leading technology companies in which it is easy to deal in a large number of shares.

    The area of technology in which British industry clearly excels is Pharmaceuticals, with Glaxo Wellcome, Zeneca and Smithkline Beecham the dominant companies. In the related Healthcare area there is Amersham International and in Support Services Misys is one of the UK's largest computer services companies, although in early 1996 it was capitalised at only £430m.

2. *Companies that are ASPIRING to becoming leading established companies*

    Electronics and Electrical Equipment companies like Psion have made great strides in recent years – in early 1996 Psion was capitalised at over £200m. Newcomers to the market like Telspec at £240m and Filtronic Comtek at £180m are also climbing the market capitalisation tables. In Support Services, Sage was ninth with a market capitalisation of £360m while Micro Focus had fallen back to under £100m.

3. *SMALL companies that have products, make profits but have yet to prove if they can last the pace and become a Psion or a Sage*

    There are plenty of small to medium-sized companies, like Cedardata, Microvitec and Kewill Systems capitalised at £40m–50m. All of them are making profits, have moderate to good records and are hoping to become major companies.

4. *Companies that make no profits yet, but are engaged in very exciting RESEARCH or have a CONCEPT that could grow explosively*

Biotech companies, like British Biotech, Biocompatibles International and ML Laboratories have exciting research programmes. Other companies like Trafficmaster and Phonelink, have a concept. These kinds of companies usually come to the market with a potentially rewarding research project or concept, raise plenty of money to fund further research and development and/or to bring their concept to commercial fruition. It is almost impossible to value their shares. They often have massive market capitalisations, which anticipate kingdom-come and sometimes well beyond.

5. *FALLEN ANGELS*

Successful growth companies in the technology sector that have had a 'glitch' – an unexpected happening that results in a major earnings setback, a drastic fall in the share price and a consequent buying opportunity.

DIFFERENT APPROACHES TO VALUATION

The approach to valuing these five different types of companies varies considerably:

1. *Leading companies*

A leading company is very much like any other growth share and is easy to value. The key factors are the multiple, the growth rate, the PEG, the cash flow, the cash position, and the long-term outlook for the industry as a whole and the company's competitive advantage within it.

2. *Aspiring companies*

An aspiring leader needs a little more care because there is a greater risk that it might stumble. More attention should be paid to the company's position in its industry, its game plan and its liquidity. Also, excessive multiples should be avoided. When and if the company becomes a leader, its multiple will tend to fall to more normal levels. If you begin to invest on a lofty 30 times earnings, and the share is likely to settle finally at say 15 times, the management would need to double EPS for the shares simply to stand still.

In essence, therefore, a share on a low PEG with a PER not too far removed from the average level is the ideal. You may think that shares like this are hard to find, but both Telspec and Filtronic Comtek had attractive PEGs in their early years, Psion and Sage have had attractive PEGs for some time now and Azlan's PEG in early 1996 was a very attractive 0.36.

3. *Small companies*

Even more caution should be used when investing in a very small technology company. If you are investing when all appears to be well, you may find that the multiple is too demanding. You always have to bear in mind that there may be a hidden problem like unforeseen obsolescence of a key product or increasing competition. With a very small company, either of these events could be sufficient to put it on the critical list, so look for low PEGs, avoid very high multiples and bear in mind that the liquidity of the company and its cash flow are particularly important.

4. *Research and concept companies*

Companies which do not make profits are the most difficult to value. They are all about hopes for the future and investors often get carried away because they tend to be hopeful people. The list of companies that have disappointed investors is sadly very long. However, when the bull becomes rampant again, they quickly forget about past disappointments and concentrate on the next road-to-riches story.

Very few of the concept-type stocks become major companies. Most of them fall by the wayside, some achieve just moderate success while others are taken over. However, new technology issues continue to appeal to investors, who are ever hopeful that they are being offered the chance to buy shares in the next Microsoft.

Before giving you a few guidelines for buying concept stocks, I would like to tell you a cautionary tale. It is about a company which came to the market while it was still losing money, had an ambitious research programme and high hopes for the future.

PROTEUS INTERNATIONAL

Proteus International became public in May 1990, at an issue price of 84p. Since then it has had a series of rights issues to fund further research and continuous losses. From 1992 to the beginning of 1994, it was highly thought of and was priced for most of that time above 400p. In early 1994, when I was asked by the London *Evening Standard* to name a share to sell short as a bear bet, I nominated Proteus. It was a good choice – by early 1996 the price had fallen to 50p.

The activities of Proteus, as described in REFS, should have been a dream for investors in high-tech. But the company seems to find it very difficult to make profits and its research expenditure burns through the proceeds of successive rights issues at an alarming rate. Americans often refer to these kinds of stocks as having a 'burn rate' – the number of years it will take them to burn through their cash before they need another rights issue.

I attended a seminar on Healthcare stocks when I was writing for the *Independent* and the shares of Proteus stood at about 400p. These were my comments in an article in April 1993. 'I was not in the least bit impressed by the presentation of Proteus International. The market capitalisation is already over £100m and the chief executive spoke like an uncommercial Martian about computer-aided molecular modelling and rational drug design. No earnings are in sight in the foreseeable future, so investors can probably look forward to a stream of announcements about new highly technical joint ventures and a series of rights issues. Not for me.'

In May 1996, there was a rescue rights issue at 45p and the company may now be on a sounder footing.

GUIDELINES FOR INVESTING IN RESEARCH AND CONCEPT STOCKS

If you are intent upon buying research and concept stocks, here are some suggested guidelines:

a. Avoid concept stocks with massive market capitalisations. Even if they succeed, their share prices have too much work to do just to stand still.

b. Avoid concept stocks that have no sales and seem to be years away from making profits. Remember that profits may never materialise and, even if they do, you might have to wait too long to make sense of your investment.

c. Avoid concept stocks that keep breaking their promises. Delays in bringing products to fruition and to commercial application are anathema to the market.

d. Make sure that concept stocks are well funded for years ahead so that the next rights issue and the one after that will not depress the shares unduly.

e. Look upon investing in concept stocks as making a series of bets. All of them are long shots so look for good odds and make more than one bet. The odds on each bet improve if the market capitalisation is relatively small and the share price is not already discounting kingdom-come. Each bet also improves if the company is in sight of making profits and has sufficient cash to last without yet another rights issue.

5. *Fallen angels*

If you like the fallen angel approach, you should read *Super Stocks*, a superb book by ace American investor, Kenneth Fisher. The book was recommended to me by Conor McCarthy, the editor of *Techinvest*, who told me that Fisher's ideas had also had a profound effect on his approach to selecting technology shares.

In essence, Fisher's philosophy is that successful growth companies in the technology sector often have a 'glitch', which can be the result of a gap between old products being phased out and new and improved products being ready to take their place. Other possible causes are teething troubles with a new product or an unfortunate acquisition.

Growth companies are often over-rated but, after a glitch, the market invariably reacts the other way, forcing the shares down to previously unplumbed depths. Meanwhile, companies that encounter these kinds of difficulties usually begin a period of internal reappraisal and reorganisation. As a result, overheads are cut, new products are developed and marketing is streamlined.

Managements also tend to take the view that, if they are going to have a break in their company's earnings record, they might as well be thorough and write off all doubtful assets and reserve against every contingency. If the company then manages to recover, it often emerges much stronger than before.

While a business is experiencing a glitch, conventional measures of valuation such as yields and PERs can be useless. When a company is making losses, it can fall into a kind of black hole in the stock market. Investors who know how to measure the value of a company, while it is in that hole, operate at a considerable advantage to those who can only play guessing games.

Before investing, it pays to wait until there have been two profit warnings. The first one is unreliable as management is often still too optimistic about recovery prospects. With the second one, provisions are usually made for every possible contingency and in the accompanying gloom the shares frequently become a buy. Absolute cynics wait for the third profit warning.

PRICE-TO-SALES RATIO

Fisher's first measure is the price-to-sales ratio (PSR): the total market value of the company divided by its sales in the last twelve months. Fisher recommends avoiding stocks on PSRs of over 1.5 and aggressively seeking out companies on PSRs of under 0.75. He clearly demonstrates in his book that high PSRs are dangerous and low ones are potentially very attractive. For further details on PSRs see Chapter 12.

PRICE-TO-RESEARCH RATIO

Fisher's second measure is the price-to-research ratio (PRR), which is the market value of the company divided by its research and development expenditure (R and D) over the last twelve months. He suggests buying companies on PRRs of between five and ten, and avoiding companies with PRRs of greater than 15.

Fisher believes the PSR is the more powerful measure, but he uses the PRR as an additional cross-check to determine whether or not a share is a buy. For example, a technology company that seems a little expensive on a sales basis could still be attractive if its PRR is exceptionally attractive. Conversely, a company with a very attractive PSR might not be spending enough on research, which would give cause for concern.

An important caveat is that the allocation of expenditure to research and development can be somewhat arbitrary; different companies may classify the same expenditure in different ways. Also a number of companies capitalise all or part of their R and D.

RESEARCH AND DEVELOPMENT EXPENDITURE

The guidance given by the Accounting Standards Board in SSAP 13 is that 'development costs may be deferred to future periods in respect of defined projects, the outcome of which can be assessed with reasonable certainty as to their technical feasibility and commercial viability. Otherwise all R and D should be written off as it is incurred.' You can readily see that words like 'reasonable certainty' offer plenty of scope for different interpretations.

Paul Taylor, in an excellent article in the *Financial Times* in July 1995, drew attention to some comments by Mr Richard Holway in an issue of his *System House* newsletter. Mr Holway made the point that Cedardata had just reported maiden pre-tax profits of £3.57m while Quality Software Products, which produces similar software, reported pre-tax profits of £2.51m. However, Cedardata, like most companies in the industry, writes off R & D as it is incurred, whereas QSP capitalises most of its R & D and amortises it over a number of years. If QSP had used the same accounting procedure as Cedardata, it would have made a loss instead of a profit. QSP believes its accounting policy makes sense because it is involved in long-term and large-scale product development. Its approach is perfectly legitimate, but you can readily see that investors have to make careful adjustments when comparing similar companies that treat R & D in different ways.

An additional complication of capitalising R & D is the effect it has on the balance sheet. In the case of QSP, in mid-1995 intangibles accounted for 90% of net assets. This is a less important worry, however, because most software companies have very low net assets in relation to their share prices, and the real value of intellectual property of this nature is very difficult to assess.

The chickens came home to roost in late January 1996 when QSP gave a profit warning for the year ended 31 December 1995. The shares fell from 608p to 490p and by early July 1996 stood at only 230p.

Other companies that capitalise R & D and were mentioned in the FT article included Computerised Financial Solutions, MAID, JBA Holdings, Micro Focus and Unipalm. JBA only capitalised R & D in relation to one product, while £13.7m was written off in the normal way. Micro Focus capitalised £9.7m and amortised £7.1m, so the net difference to profits was only £2.6m. In contrast, MAID capitalised £2.3m and only wrote off £133,000, so the difference of over £2.1m transformed the actual loss of £1.16m for the year ended 31 December 1994 into a reported profit of over £1m. In the following financial year MAID lost £4.4m.

The other adverse effect of capitalising R & D is that it boosts the year's cash flow per share. Instead of reducing cash flow, the R & D expenditure in question is added to capital expenditure. To obtain a better picture of this kind of technology share, I recommend deducting capital expenditure from cash flow to give a shorthand version of Warren Buffett's famous 'owners' earnings' per share. In the case of JBA, for example, 1994 cash flow of –11.4p per share was increased by capital expenditure of 21.2p to –32.6p per share. In the case of MAID, 1994 positive cash flow of 2.01p was obliterated by capital expenditure of 4.49p to give owners' earnings of –2.48p per share.

The obvious message for any investor in technology stocks is to read the annual accounts carefully to determine whether or not R & D is being capitalised and, if so, to what extent. To be consistent, it is then better to adjust the figures to show what the profits or losses would have been with R & D written off completely. Only by doing this can valid comparisons be made between similar companies in the same industry. I hasten to add that on some occasions there may be very good reasons for capitalising expenditure and I am sure that the directors of all of the companies I have mentioned believed that it was right and proper to do so. However, *the investor has to adopt a consistent approach and a safe one*. It is certainly consistent to compare companies' profits or losses adjusted to the same basis, with R & D written off in all cases, and it is unquestionably safer to work on this more conservative assumption. Fisher's approach for buying technology stocks also errs very much on the side of safety, as his aim is to identify shares at bargain-basement prices.

PROFIT MARGINS

Fisher's methods work best with companies that, in normal circumstances, have a distinct advantage over their competitors. After the PSR and PRR, his third measure is to make a very detailed study of profit margins, which are the essential ingredient that transforms sales into bottom-line earnings. When and if a company recovers from a glitch, those earnings form the basis for calculating PERs again. As the company comes out of the black hole, the share price then begins to improve, often dramatically.

In America, the analysis of profit margins is more of an exact science, because company managements tend to talk more freely with investment analysts. Fisher makes a number of suggestions on the best way to approach margin analysis, but it has to be borne in mind that he was writing his book *Super Stocks* primarily for the American market. Although his approach to margins would be difficult to emulate in the UK, it is worth studying his suggestions carefully to understand his thinking. His key points are as follows:

1. Fisher looks for companies with an unfair advantage that may arise from distribution, scale, trade secrets, a quality image, a low cost base or a substantial lead time. In essence, Fisher means a competitive advantage. One of the best ways of checking this quickly is to compare the margins of the company under review with the margins of all the other similar companies in its sector and with the sector average.

2. To determine margins, Fisher suggests asking management what they expect their company's margins will be in the current year and beyond. In the US, managers will often tell you in a frank and open way. Fisher then suggests asking them how their goals are going to be achieved – by more efficient manufacturing, product planning, lower costs or whatever. The quality of the answers sometimes gives a clue as to the credibility of management's projections.

3. Fisher recommends being sceptical of claims that margins will improve simply by doing old things a little better. He suggests that careful attention should be paid to the track record of the

CEO, especially in relation to the margins and profits of their previous companies.

4. He attaches a lot of importance to market share. The more the better.

5. Finally, Fisher warns about the danger of judging margins by purely domestic benchmarks – international competition or the threat of it has to be taken into account.

EXAMPLES OF USING FISHER'S APPROACH

What I like about Fisher's approach is the courage his key ratios (PSR, PRR and profit margins) give investors during periods when companies have had glitches and are in black holes. Obviously, there will be a failure rate, but when the approach works it often produces what Peter Lynch so aptly describes as 'a tenbagger' – a share that rises in value ten-fold. The few losses you might experience should be more than offset by the occasional spectacular gain.

I asked Conor McCarthy to give me a good example of *Techinvest*'s success using Fisher's approach. He mentioned Kewill Systems, which went astray a few years ago by making an unfortunate acquisition in Germany. The company began to make substantial losses and the shares fell from 318p in 1992 to a low of 49p in 1993. At this point, the PRR of 2 was astoundingly attractive. The German subsidiary was sold shortly afterwards and by the end of 1993 Kewill Systems had risen to 265p.

Conor McCarthy has found that *Techinvest*'s greatest successes have been achieved by buying shares with PRRs of under 5.0 coupled with PSRs of under 0.5. The tables in every monthly issue of REFS show those companies with the lowest PRRs in each of the indices together with details of cash flow, the PSR and the trend of both margins and sales.

ESSENTIAL READING

In Chapter 19 on Recommended Reading, I have set out all of the newsletters and books that I recommend to investors together with details of how to get hold of them. However, I will also highlight here those publications that are of crucial importance to investors in technology stocks:

Techinvest (£99 rising to £139 per annum in subsequent years) is the leading technology newsletter and an absolute must for growth investors who are interested in technology stocks.

System House (£295 per annum) is another exceptional newsletter. It does not recommend investments, but gives invaluable background information on the financial performance of most companies in the computing services industry. *System House* has been very prescient in seeing the tremendous scope for growth in the industry and often gives excellent advice of a general nature as well as reviewing the results of individual companies and highlighting important issues like the capitalisation of R & D.

The Holway Report (£1750) is a comprehensive annual report on the computing services industry with substantial background information on the main companies. This tome contains a great deal of comparative analysis and should be of positive assistance to institutions and private investors with very sizeable technology portfolios.

Super Stocks (£14.99), by Kenneth Fisher, is in my view the best investment book on technology stocks that has ever been written. The author explains in detail his techniques for identifying 'super stocks' and for buying them after they have had a glitch, at bargain-basement prices. A compelling and instructive read for enthusiastic investors in the technology sector.

SUMMARY

1. There are five main types of technology stock:

   a) *Leading* established companies.

   b) *Aspiring* leaders.

   c) *Small* companies with products and profits.

   d) *Research and Concept* stocks that do not yet have profits and often do not have any proven products.

e) *Fallen angels*

2. The approaches to valuing the five different types of technology stock vary:

a) *Leading companies*

A conventional approach is called for – the competitive advantage, multiple, growth rate, cash position and long-term outlook are the crucial measures.

b) *Aspiring companies*

The same approach as for the leaders, but more attention to be paid to the company's position in its industry, its game plan and its liquidity. Avoid excessive multiples.

c) *Small companies*

The usual investment measures apply, but even more caution is needed. Look for low PEGs, avoid high multiples and put even stronger emphasis on cash flow and liquidity.

d) *Concept stocks*

My suggested guidelines are as follows:

1. Avoid massive market capitalisations.

2. Avoid companies with no present sales and those that are years away from making profits.

3. Avoid managements that keep breaking their promises.

4. Make sure that the companies are well funded.

5. Look upon investing in concept stocks as a series of bets. On every bet you should try to improve the odds by following the above guidelines.

e) *Fallen angels*

Watch for a glitch and look for companies which appear to

have a good chance of recovery and have PSRs of under 0.75 and PRRs of between 5 and 10. It usually pays to wait for at least two profit warnings. Operating margins are also of great importance. Fisher's approach on margins is as follows. He:

1. Likes companies with a competitive advantage.

2. Talks to management about its goals for margins.

3. Recommends being sceptical about extravagant claims of changes in the margins of old businesses.

4. Checks CEOs' track records of margins in their previous businesses.

5. Likes strong market share.

6. Warns about the threat of international competition and the danger of judging companies' margins purely domestically.

3. Always check how technology companies treat their R & D expenditure. Beware of those that capitalise it. If the company does capitalise R & D, I recommend reworking the figures to show the effect of writing it off each year.

4. For serious investors in technology stocks, *Techinvest* is a monthly must. *System House* is highly desirable, if it can be afforded, and *The Holway Report* is strongly recommended to institutional investors and really substantial private investors.

The book *Super Stocks* by Kenneth Fisher is superb and gives a real insight into how to buy technology stocks at bargain-basement prices.

18

CYCLICAL STOCKS

This book is primarily about growth stocks, but a chapter has been spared for cyclicals as all companies are cyclical to a greater or lesser extent. The term 'cyclicals' usually refers to those stocks that are particularly sensitive to the ups and downs of the economy as a whole.

One of the biggest single influences on the economy is the level and trend of interest rates. Cyclical stocks benefit most when interest rates are falling as, in due course, that usually stimulates the economy. Conversely, in times of rising interest rates, cyclical stocks fare very badly.

All companies do better when the economy is prospering and find the going tough when it is in the doldrums. However, even in the worst trading conditions, great growth companies still manage to turn in increased earnings per share year after year. Their rate of growth may be slower than their long-term average, but growth will still be a continuing feature. In contrast, cyclicals, such as steel producers, paper manufacturers, automobile manufacturers, housebuilders and chemical companies, react more violently to changes in interest rates. Often they make substantial losses during severe depressions and have difficulty in surviving until the next boom. When and if they finally recover, the swing from losses to profits is often far in excess of expectations.

I much prefer growth stocks as a steady diet, but there is no doubt that in some years cyclicals outperform them by a wide margin. Fortunately for me this happens infrequently, but when cyclicals are in vogue it can be very hard going for growth investors to produce their usual outperformance.

Pinning down exactly when it pays to invest in cyclicals is obviously crucial. Credit Lyonnais Laing, the stockbroker, prepared a very interesting circular in late 1994, setting out the circumstances required for cyclicals to outperform non-cyclicals. The table below is an extract from their excellent research:

	Performance Relative to Industrials		Interest Rate Trend	Sterling Effective Rate Trend	Non-Oil GDP Growth (Q4 y-o-y)
	Non-Cyclicals %	Domestic Cyclicals %			%
1980	+10.4	−11.2	Falling	Rising	−7.3
1981	+9.3	−11.5	Rising	Falling	+1.7
1982	+7.0	−1.0	Falling	Falling	+2.2
1983	−5.4	+12.8	Falling	Rising	+4.5
1984	+6.1	−7.1	Rising	Falling	+1.8
1985	−4.1	−2.5	Falling	Rising	+3.4
1986	+2.0	+1.4	Falling	Falling	+4.1
1987	−4.1	+0.2	Falling	Rising	+5.3
1988	+1.7	−7.1	Rising	Rising	+3.5
1989	+11.2	−16.2	Rising	Falling	+1.8
1990	+2.2	−11.6	Falling	Rising	−0.5
1991	+8.7	−14.8	Falling	Falling	−1.9
1992	+1.5	−9.1	Falling	Falling	0.2
1993	−13.1	+26.2	Falling	Rising	2.3
1994	−1.6	−1.1	Rising	Falling	3.0

As you can see, the best years for cyclicals were 1983 (+12.8% against −5.4%), 1985 (−2.5% against −4.1%), 1987 (+0.2% against −4.1%) and 1993 (+26.2% against −13.1%). In the other eleven years cyclicals underperformed non-cyclicals, emphasising that to be successful with cyclicals, it is vitally important to get your timing absolutely right.

The CLL circular shows that falling interest rates were a key factor common to the four most successful years for cyclicals. Looked at the other way around, there was no year of rising interest rates in which cyclicals performed well.

In three of the four best years for cyclicals, you can also see how they performed relatively well in the *last* year of falling interest rates before they began to rise again.

In all four of the best years for cyclicals, sterling was also rising. It is, of course, easy to tell when sterling is rising and when interest rates are falling. The difficult point to ascertain is whether or not it is the *last* year of falling interest rates. Possibly the best way of determining this is to check if GDP non-oil growth is at a relatively high level. Certainly, the 4.5% growth in 1983 and the 5.3% growth in 1987 would have flashed a warning signal that falling interest rates were at an end and a rise was imminent.

In the best three years for cyclicals, 1983, 1987 and 1993, interest rates had already fallen during the previous year and in 1987 and 1993 for several years before. It seems therefore that the first year of falling interest rates is unlikely to be right for cyclicals. 1985 was a minor exception, but their outperformance was so trivial that it can be ignored.

To summarise the general factors needed for well-timed investment in cyclicals:

1. The second or subsequent year of falling interest rates seems to be a far better bet than the first year.

2. Sterling should be rising.

3. The last year of falling interest rates is optimum. If growth in non-oil GDP rises to 4% or more, this seems to be an obvious signal that higher interest rates are likely in the following year.

MORE GUIDELINES FOR BUYING CYCLICALS

Before selecting a cyclical share, it is probably a better idea to pick an industry that is due for a rebound. The second step is to pick one or more companies that seem to be particularly attractive. The largest companies in the industry are likely to be safest; the smaller ones will usually offer the biggest percentage gains but they are also far more likely to go to the wall.

Peter Lynch says that when considering whether or not to buy shares in, for example, a leading copper producer, he would prefer the opinion of a plumber who knows what is happening to copper prices, to that of an MBA who thinks the shares are a buy because they look cheap. In fact, the lower the multiple of a cyclical, the more dangerous it is to buy – a share that looks cheap may in fact be very dear indeed. A very high multiple usually signals the bottom of the cycle, whereas a very low one can be a warning that the end of the upturn is nigh.

RELATIVE STRENGTH

When investing in cyclicals you want the industry and your chosen company within it to be surrounded by gloom and doom. The PER may be very high, but the newsflow could be beginning to turn positive and the relative strength of the shares should be beginning to pick up. If this is happening, it often pays to grit your teeth and pay up to get hold of the stock.

CASH POSITION

There is another very important fundamental factor to consider – the strength of the company's balance sheet. A substantial positive cash position is obviously very reassuring, as is strong cash flow. However, even if the company has massive borrowings, it may still be all right provided the newsflow is turning really positive. A rights issue may be necessary, but at least the company should survive.

The time to really worry about inadequate cash is if you buy into a recovery stock when trading conditions are still deteriorating or, at best, static. I do not recommend this approach, but some investors shoot for a really big gain by trying to invest right at the bottom. If you are determined to play cyclicals this way, I suggest that you at least ensure that the company's balance sheet is strong. This will give you a longer time to be proved right.

OTHER FINANCIAL STATISTICS

With a cyclical, the price-to-book value is always of interest. The net assets of the company are the raw material to fuel the recovery. Obviously, any company standing at a substantial premium to its book value is far less attractive than one standing at a massive discount.

Similarly, a very low price-to-sales ratio gives an excellent indication of the scope for future recovery when the industry picks up and margins begin to improve. For this reason, it is always worth trying to establish normal peak margins for the sector and to compare them with present levels.

BRITISH STEEL

The two charts and sets of key statistics are taken from the REFS company entries for British Steel in March 1995 and March 1996. As

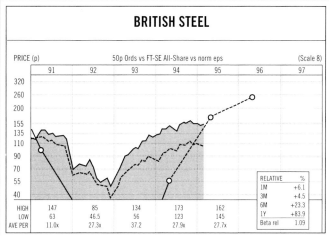

BRITISH STEEL

PRICE (p) — 50p Ords vs FT-SE All-Share vs norm eps — (Scale 8)

	91	92	93	94	95	96	97
HIGH	147	85	134	173	162		
LOW	63	46.5	56	123	145		
AVE PER	11.0x	27.3x	37.2	27.9x	27.7x		

RELATIVE %
1M +6.1
3M +4.5
6M +23.3
1Y +83.9
Beta rel 1.09

PRICE (NMS 100) 27-FEB-95	**159p**
norm eps (pr)	23.6p
market cap	£3,209m
turnover (94AR)	£4,191m
pretax (94AR)	£80.0m

			m	s
DY (pr)	%	5.99	●	●
PER (pr)	x	6.74	●	●
PEG (pr)	f	na		
GR (pr)	%	52.2	●	●
ROCE	%	4.15		●
MARGIN	%	3.56		●
GEAR	%	-1.44	●	●
PBV	x	0.85	●	●
PTBV	x	0.85	●	●
PCF	x	10.5	●	●
PSR	x	0.76	●	●
PRR	x	na		

FT-SE 100	44th
market overall	45th

ACTIVITIES: Manufacture and sale of steel. TEL: (0171) 735 7654.
REGISTRAR: Lloyds, Worthing. Tel: (01903) 502541. **BROKERS:** Cazenove. UBS.
OUTLOOK: (20-Jun-94) AR: ch & ce – "...the improvement in the UK economic outlook should impact favourably on results as will the full year benefit of selling price increases implemented during the course of last year". (27-Jul-94) **AGM:** no outlook statement. (14-Nov-94) Int: ch & ce – "Prospects for the second half are encouraging. Steel demand in the UK and continental Europe is expected to grow by some 5%".

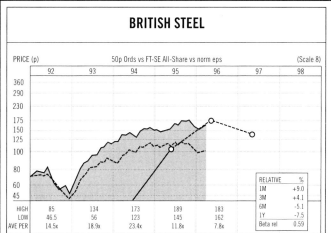

BRITISH STEEL

PRICE (p) — 50p Ords vs FT-SE All-Share vs norm eps — (Scale 8)

	92	93	94	95	96	97	98
HIGH	85	134	173	189	183		
LOW	46.5	56	123	145	162		
AVE PER	14.5x	18.9x	23.4x	11.8x	7.8x		

RELATIVE %
1M +9.0
3M +4.1
6M -5.1
1Y -7.5
Beta rel 0.59

PRICE (NMS 100) 26-FEB-96	**183p**
norm eps (pr)	28.9p
turnover (95AR)	£4,784m
pretax (95AR)	£578m

			m	s
DY (pr)	%	6.75	●	●
PER (pr)	x	6.32	●	●
PEG (pr)	f	na		
GR (pr)	%	na		
ROCE	%	12.2	●	●
MARGIN	%	8.80	●	●
GEAR	%	-3.16	●	●
PBV	x	0.90	●	●
PTBV	x	0.90	●	●
PCF	x	8.07	●	●
PSR	x	0.77	●	●
PRR	x	na		

market cap	£3,715m
position	50th
FT-SE 100	

ACTIVITIES: Manufacture and sale of steel. TEL: (0171) 735 7654.
REGISTRAR: Lloyds, Worthing. Tel: (01903) 502541. **BROKERS:** Cazenove. UBS.
INTERIM: (13-Nov-95) ½ yr to 30 Sep 95. T/O £3,611m (£2,819m). Pre tax profit £550m (£159m). EPS 19.3p (6.49p). Int div 3.00p (2.00p). **OUTLOOK:** (19-Jun-95) AR: ch & ce – "Whilst there may be little sign of recovery in consumer confidence in the UK, many of our customers, particularly those exporting, are experiencing better levels of activity and are generally more optimistic". (26-Jul-95) **AGM:** ch – "...I expect 1995/96 to show considerable improvement on last year". (13-Nov-95) Int: ch & ce – "Steel demand in the second half is expected to be less strong than in the first half although underlying consumption of steel remains satisfactory in most markets".

you can see from the dotted line, the brokers' consensus forecast changed for the worse during the year.

In spite of very attractive key statistics in March 1995 (a dividend yield of 5.99%, a PER of only 6.74, net cash, a PSR of 0.76, good cash flow and a discount to book value) relative strength for the following year was poor. In March 1996, EPS for the year ahead were forecast to decline so future newsflow was likely to turn negative. Even with such attractive fundamentals, British Steel shares were only for the brave.

NEWSFLOW

I have mentioned a few times the magic word 'newsflow'. It does not only refer to announcements about profits and dividends. It also embraces such items as factories being sold or closed, major redundancies, large orders being secured, appointments of new directors and the like. A new chief executive can often be a major turning point for a company: Archie Norman at Asda, Gerry Robinson at Granada and Lord Wolfson and David Jones at Next, to name but a few. However, newsflow does not have to be so dramatic; it just needs to be becoming more and more positive. It is the trend of newsflow that is the main influence on the share price.

DIRECTORS' BUYING

As always, a cluster of directors buying a significant number of shares is very encouraging. With a cyclical it is arguably even more of an endorsement than usual. If the company is, in trading terms, right at its low, there is a risk of it failing altogether. In that event, the directors would lose their jobs as well as the capital they have already invested in the company's shares. To add to their downside risk, by buying further shares, shows that they are very confident indeed that the company will recover fully.

SUMMARY

1. The factors needed for a well-timed investment in cyclicals are as follows:

    a) The second or subsequent year of falling interest rates seems to be a far better bet than the first year.

b) Sterling should be rising.

c) The last year of falling interest rates is optimum. If growth in non-oil GDP rises to 4% or more, the chances are that interest rates will rise in the following year.

2. Do not buy cyclicals blind. Try to find someone who is in the industry or knows a lot about it. Read as much general information as possible about the industry.

3. Treat low multiples with caution. They may indicate trouble on the horizon.

4. Do not be frightened of high multiples provided the news from the company is beginning to turn, even very slightly. The trend of future newsflow will be the main influence on the share price.

5. Prefer companies with a strong cash position or one that is improving quickly.

6. A substantial discount to book value and a low PSR can be encouraging indications of the scope for future recovery.

7. Watch the relative strength of the shares carefully. If this is beginning to turn positive, it is usually an excellent sign, especially after a major downturn and long period of consolidation at the lower level.

8. As always, a cluster of directors buying shares is a very encouraging sign.

9. If all the other factors are in place, do not hesitate to pay up to buy the shares of your choice.

19

RECOMMENDED READING

Daily, weekly and monthly reading is an important aid to the effective management of any portfolio. The bare minimum for serious investors is the *Financial Times* every day, at least one other good daily, one leading Sunday paper and the *Investors Chronicle* every week.

In addition to daily papers, technical and trade magazines in the areas in which you specialise, or have an interest, can often give you an edge over other investors.

It is obviously desirable to read as much as possible about investment, but most investors have restricted budgets. The size of your budget will be determined by the size of your portfolio, but be prepared to spend more than you might at first think is sensible. The right information will repay the original cost many times over.

During the last two decades, the market as a whole has risen on average by well over 12% per annum excluding dividends. Although only a very small number of professional fund managers seem to be able to beat the market on a regular basis, I believe that doubling the market's performance is a sensible target for private investors. You only need to study the results of the back-tests REFS made on shares with low PEGs, high relative strength and strong cash flow to see that on average the market's performance was more than trebled. Of course, the back-tests need to be made over a much longer period, but logic dictates that shares with a proven record growing their EPS at a much faster rate than the average, coupled with better cash flow and better relative strength, should continue to outperform the market by a wide margin.

It is, of course, possible to ask your broker to provide you with lists of shares that fulfill these and other criteria. The right broker will be able to do this with ease. If, however, you prefer to select your own shares, REFS is the obvious answer.

If an investor could double the performance of the market by using REFS and other investment aids, then on a £100,000 portfolio an extra

£10,000-worth* of capital profits could be generated in an average year. Capital gains tax would, of course, need to be deducted for any gains outside PEPs and the tax-free allowance. However, it is conservative to assume that one-fifth of the extra 10% performance – two per cent of the portfolio value – should be set aside for investment aids if the money being spent helps to produce the improved results and continues to do so.

Two per cent of a portfolio worth £25,000 would allow £500 total expenditure, which easily affords a quarterly copy of REFS with £250 to spare for other products. On a £50,000 portfolio about £1,000 is the right amount and on £100,000 about £2,000. With a portfolio of between £50,000 and £100,000 it would be worthwhile to switch to the monthly version of REFS. The extra benefits should more than compensate for the extra cost.

With portfolios of between £100,000 and £500,000, I suggest about 0.5% on the excess over £100,000 should be added to the £2,000 yearly sum. On a portfolio of £300,000, this would mean spending about £3,000 and on £500,000 about £4,000. For portfolios of above £500,000 the relative cost of supplementary investment aids is no longer an important factor – if they help, buy them.

An easy way to afford more investment aids than would be justified by an individual's portfolio is to join a well-run investment club with a sizeable portfolio. Together, the members should easily be able to afford products like REFS, *Analyst* and *Techinvest*. It would also be a very good idea for the club to found an investment library. To get it started, all members could contribute a book that they have already read, and subsequently new ones could be bought using the club's funds.

Bearing budgets in mind, I have set out below my suggestions for additional reading and information in an order loosely based on the improvement to investment performance each is likely to provide. The subscription prices mentioned are those prevailing in June 1996.

COMPANY REFS is the full name of the product; the acronym REFS stands for Really Essential Financial Statistics. The publication is available both monthly and quarterly and provides private and

---

*For the 10 years ended 31 December 1993, for example, the market enjoyed an average annual return of 18.8% including dividends. In an average year, 10% excluding dividends therefore seems to me a reasonable and conservative basis to work on.

institutional investors with the financial statistics and other information about companies that they really need to know. There is a full-page entry for all quoted UK companies other than investment trusts, and a half-page entry for all AIM companies. The full-page entry includes the rolling twelve months ahead PER, dividend yield, growth rate and PEG, the return on capital employed, margin, price-to-sales ratio, price-to-cash flow, price-to-research and development ratio, price-to-book value and gearing. There are also five-year details of normalised EPS, FRS3 EPS, tax rates, cash flow per share, capital expenditure, dividends per share, sales per share, margin, ROCE, depreciation and interest.

Another panel shows the normalised EPS consensus forecast, together with details of the individual brokers' contributions to it and their buy, sell or hold recommendations. A further panel analyses the company's gearing in detail and shows interest and dividend cover, together with the quick and current ratios. Share capital is set out clearly, together with details of the directors' holdings and an indication of whether they have sold or bought during the last six months. There is also a chart of the share price, relative strength and EPS growth coupled with the share price's highs and lows and the average PER over each of the last five years. A further panel analyses the company's turnover and profit both geographically and by activity and the outlook statement shows the last few price-sensitive comments by the chairman. There is also an extensive panel showing the pertinent points from newsflow over the previous year.

The company entry contains so much information that it is impossible to do it justice by words alone. A typical entry for Medeva on 29 May 1996 is therefore set out lifesize on pages 190 and 191. It has been split in two as it would not fit on one page of this book: brokers' estimates and gearing, cover always appear at the bottom of each page of the REFS companies volume.

Although the company entry is comprehensive, REFS provides much more. A tables volume shows, index by index, the contenders for promotion and demotion, shares with the highest and lowest relative strength, highest yields, lowest PEGs, highest and lowest PERs, best cash flows, best returns on capital employed, best price-to-book values and much more.

In addition, there is an analysis of each sector showing how the detailed statistics of each company compare with the other companies in its peer group and with the sector and the market averages. There

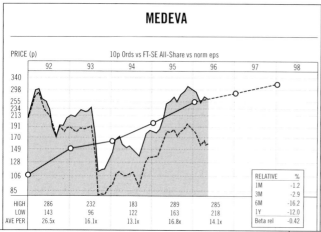

MEDEVA

SEDOL:	575650	**REUTER:**	MDV.L
EPIC:	MDV	**BLMBRG:**	MDV

PRICE (NMS 25)
29-MAY-96   24◂

market cap		£7Σ
position		19
index		FT-SE Mid
norm eps (pr)		2C
turnover (95AR)		£2Σ
pretax (95AR)		£79

ACTIVITIES ANALYSIS (95AR)

		T/O	Pr
Pharmaceutical products	%	100	100
UK	%	21	15
Rest of Europe	%	12	7
USA	%	64	79
Rest of the World	%	2	

				m
DY (pr)	%	2.50		⊟
PER (pr)	x	12.2		⬤
PEG (pr)	f	1.23		⬤
GR (pr)	%	10.0		⬤
ROCE	%	78.4		⬤
MARGIN	%	31.7		⬤
GEAR	%	-6.25		⬤
PBV	x	4.80		⊟
PTBV	x	7.23		⊟
PCF	x	16.2		⬤
PSR	x	2.77		◀
PRR	x	41.9		◀

nav ps (95AR)   50
net cash ps (95AR)   3.2

SECTOR: Pharmaceuticals. **ACTIVITIES:** Development, manufacture and sale of prescription pharmaceutical products.

DIRS: J W Baker (ch)*, Dr W Bogie (ce), G Watts (fd), G H Schulze, Dr M D Young, K B Sinclair*, M F Julien, B Rigby*. **HEAD & REG OFF:** 10 St James's Street, London, SW1A 1EF. Tel: (0171) 839 3888. Fax: (0171) 930 1514. **REGISTRAR:** IRG, Witham. Tel: (01376) 515755

BROKERS: de Zoete & Bevan; Panmure Gordon. **FINANCIAL ADVISERS:** Lazard Bros. **AUDITORS:** KPMG.

OUTLOOK: (19-Feb-96) AR: ch - "The outlook for further significant growth for Medeva is good - the company is in a healthy state...its prospects remain bright". (25-Apr-96) AGM: ch - "...trading for the group as a whole is in line with management's expectations".

NEWSFLOW: (29-Jun-95) Ann: The company has agreed to acquire the intellectual property and US distribution rights for the tetanus/diptheria vaccines currently manufactured by the Wyeth-Ayerst Laboratories Division of American Home Products. (11-Jul-95) Ann: Medeva announces that discussions with Fisons regarding a possible merger have been terminated. (19-Sep-95) Ann: The company has agreed to the repurchase by Matrix Inc of the marketing rights to AccuSite. Medeva will receive £2.00m under the agreement. (24-Oct-95) Ann: Medeva announces the acquisition from Glaxo Wellcome S.A. in Spain of the exclusive Spanish marketing rights to 7 products for a consideration of £12.4m. (22-Nov-95) Ann: Medeva has agreed to acquire Tillotts Pharma AG, Switzerland, for a consideration of SwFr18.1m (£10.1m). (22-Dec-95) Ann: An agreement has been signed with Janssen Pharmacutica International for the co-development and distribution of Medeva's hepatitis B Vaccine in the Asia-Pacific region, excluding Japan. (6-Feb-96) Ann: Medeva PLC, announces the disposal of its German operation, trading as Ribosepharm, to Klinge Pharma GmbH for a consideration of £53.8m. (20-Feb-96) Ann: ML Laboratories PLC has entered into an agreement with Medeva relating to the commercialisation of the first two products developed for ML's breath activated dry powder inhaler. (20-May-96) Ann: Medeva has acquired the US rights to the antihistamine/decongestant product, Semprex-D, from Glaxo Wellcome for $16.5m (£10.9m).

SHARE CAPITAL, HOLDINGS, DEALINGS

(1) 297m 10p Ords (Maj 22.0%, Dirs 0.03% [d]); (2) ADR.

General Electric Inv Corp	%	7.60
Scottish Widows Fund & Life	%	6.37
Franklin Resources Inc	%	5.00
Standard Life Assurance Co	%	3.01

Dr W Bogie (ce)	k	31.3	4+
G Watts (fd)	k	1.00	
J W Baker* (ch)	k	2.00	4+
Dr M D Young	k	20.00	
K B Sinclair*	k	16.6	

year ended 31 Dec		1991	1992	1993	1994	1995	**1996E**	19
turnover	£m	82.4	144	200	240	256		
depreciation	£m	3.13	5.55	9.10	14.5	14.5		
int paid (net)	£m	-0.84	1.32	1.10	-0.40	-0.90		
FRS3 pretax	£m	16.7	36.0	46.1	64.2	79.0		
norm pretax	£m	16.7	34.8	46.1	64.2	82.2	**92.4**	
turnover ps	£	0.49	0.70	0.79	0.87	0.88		
op margin	%	19.3	25.0	23.6	26.6	31.7		
ROCE	%	31.4	49.1	40.8	82.1	78.4		
ROE	%	18.2	31.6	23.0	30.4	34.2		
FRS3 eps	p	7.94	11.7	11.4	13.8	16.4		
IIMR eps	p	7.94	10.5	11.4	13.8	16.4		
norm eps	p	7.94	10.5	11.4	13.8	17.4	**19.2**	
norm eps growth	%	+144	+32.2	+8.57	+21.1	+26.4	**+9.85**	+1
tax rate	%	18	30	36	38	38	**38**	
norm per	x					14.0	**12.7**	1
cash flow ps	p	4.52	7.57	13.2	20.3	15.0		
capex ps	p	4.63	18.5	8.28	3.98	3.61		
dividend ps	p	1.43	2.15	2.70	3.30	4.00	**4.59**	Σ
dps growth	%	+98.6	+50.4	+25.6	+22.2	+21.2	**+14.8**	+1
dividend yield	%					2.05	**2.35**	Σ
dividend cover	x	5.55	4.88	4.22	4.18	4.36	**4.17**	4
shrholders funds	£m	73.9	72.8	130	132	150		
net borrowings	£m	-37.9	40.5	-5.80	-9.60	-9.40		
net curr assets	£m	25.7	-5.54	25.1	25.0	38.3		
ntav ps	p	23.7	13.2	29.8	26.8	33.8		

er	Date	Rec	1996 ESTIMATES			1997 ESTIMATES		
			Pretax £m	Eps p	Dps p	Pretax £m	Eps p	Dps p
va Europe	31-Mar-95	ADD r	83.0 r	17.4 r	4.20 r			
ings	27-Jul-95	HOLD	95.0	18.7	4.60	105	21.8	5.10
ͻ Europe	17-Jan-96	HOLD –	96.8 +	19.7 –	4.60	104	21.4	5.00
	20-Feb-96	BUY	90.4	19.5	4.50	106	22.9	5.27
	20-Feb-96	BUY	90.0	18.5 +	4.80	100	20.5	5.50
ams de Broe	28-Feb-96	BUY	90.0 –	19.2 –	4.50 –	100	20.3	5.00
ill Lynch	29-Feb-96	ACCU –	99.5 –	20.8 –	4.90 +	120	25.1	5.90
Vest Securities	29-Feb-96	RED	94.0	19.6	4.70	103	21.3	5.10
nan Brothers	6-Mar-96	OUTP	89.9	18.8	4.60	102	21.4	
mure Gordon	15-Mar-96	BUY	95.0	19.7	4.50 –	110	22.8	5.00
C James Capel	18-Mar-96	HOLD	95.0 +	19.2 +	4.80 +	103 –	20.1 –	5.50 +
Warburg	21-Mar-96	HOLD	89.0 +	18.9 +	4.70 +	112 +	23.3 +	5.50 +
T	25-Mar-96	H/B	88.5 –	18.0 –	4.40 –	100	20.0	4.90
mon	9-Apr-96	HOLD	94.0	18.8	4.70	115	22.0	5.40
it Lyonnais Laing	11-Apr-96	BUY	94.0	19.0	4.80	103	20.8	5.50
g Middleton	15-Apr-96	BUY	88.0 –	18.4 –	4.50 –	97.0	20.2	5.10
Consensus	**WBUY**		**92.4**	**19.2**	**4.59**	**103**	**21.1**	**5.27**
1M change			+0.09	+0.08	–0.05	–2.21	–0.41	–0.01
3M change			–1.74	–0.42	–0.29	–3.21	–0.80	–0.06

GEARING, COVER (95AR)

intangibles		Incl	Excl
net gearing	%	-6.25	-9.42
cash	%	8.58	12.9
gross gearing	%	2.33	3.51
under 5 yrs	%	2.33	3.51
under 1 yr	%	1.26	1.90
quick ratio	r		1.06
current ratio	r		1.44
interest cover	x		114

KEY DATES

next AR year end	31-Dec-96
int xd (1.10p)	12-Sep-94
fin xd (2.20p)	20-Mar-95
int results	19-Jul-95
int xd (1.40p)	31-Jul-95
year end	31-Dec-95
annual report	19-Feb-96
fin xd (2.60p)	1-Mar-96
agm	25-Apr-96

are also details of the last six months of directors' dealings showing the shares bought or sold together with the position of the director in question and his or her residual shareholding. Another section shows CEO changes during the preceding twelve months and another shows, index by index, monthly changes to brokers' consensus forecasts in order of magnitude.

I could go on and on but, as I devised the product and have an ongoing influence on its design and content, I have to admit that I am very biased indeed. REFS has transformed my own investment performance and Hemmington Scott now has scores of unsolicited testimonials from private investors who are delighted with it. In early 1996, the quarterly version cost £250 per annum and the monthly version £675. If you want to obtain the details, telephone 0171 278 7769 or write to the publisher, Hemmington Scott Publishing Limited, City Innovation Centre, 26–31 Whiskin Street, London EC1R OBP.

THE ESTIMATE DIRECTORY (TED) gives full coverage of individual brokers' forecasts. I would have strongly recommended investors to subscribe to TED prior to REFS supplying similar details. However, as in June 1996 the annual subscription to TED on a monthly basis was £495, it is obviously a much better proposition to pay an extra £180 per annum to subscribe instead to REFS and to obtain the brokers' estimates and all of the extra information provided in the REFS company and tables volumes. A similar argument applies to the quarterly versions – REFS is available for £250 per annum against £170 for TED.

A vital point to bear in mind is that brokers' estimates are only a *small* part of the overall equation, when deciding whether or not to buy a particular share. The REFS company entry shows *all* the statistics needed to make a valuation, including the brokers' estimates *in their full and proper setting.*

THE HAMBRO COMPANY GUIDE is an excellent quarterly publication, again from Hemmington Scott (details as above), that gives five-year profits and earnings per share figures for most UK quoted companies. There are also brief details of the balance sheet, gearing, return on capital employed, activities and key dates for announcements. Future earnings per share forecasts are covered in most cases with the consensus figure and details of the number of brokers contributing, together with the standard deviation between their estimates. The annual subscription is £115, which makes the publication ideal for private investors who feel that they cannot justify spending £250 per annum on quarterly REFS.

ANALYST is an excellent monthly publication, which has many interesting in-depth articles each month on investment systems and approaches as well as excellent growth company profiles and very detailed commentaries on small to medium-sized growth companies. There are usually special offers for first-year subscribers – in June 1996, for example, they would only have had to pay £90 in their first year, rising to £120 thereafter. Telephone: 0171 247 4557.

TECHINVEST is a monthly investment newsletter which concentrates on high-technology companies. The track record of its average recommendation is excellent and its model portfolios have performed extremely well. Most of its investment recommendations are for small to medium-sized companies, but a few reach into the Mid-250 index. The annual subscription for first-time subscribers is £99 rising to £139 in subsequent years. The publisher's address is Techinvest, Mill House, Millbrook, Naas, Co. Kildare, Ireland.

THE QUANTUM LEAP STOCKMARKET LETTER is another excellent monthly newsletter that concentrates on super-growth stocks. It is edited by Quentin Lumsden, who also writes in the *Independent on Sunday* and has a knack for identifying shares with very high compound rates of growth. The annual subscription for the first year is £69.50, rising to £99.50 in subsequent years. The publisher's address is Letterprint Ltd, P.O. Box 1638, London W8 4QR.

THE SMALL COMPANY SHAREWATCH is well worth the annual subscription of £49.50 rising to £99 in the second and subsequent years. The monthly issue contains profiles of attractive situations, updates and plenty of good ideas. The address for subscriptions is Equitylink Ltd, 75 High Street, Chislehurst, Kent BR7 5A6 (Tel: 0181 656 4648).

THE INVESTORS STOCKMARKET WEEKLY recommends five or six shares a week and touches on another two or three stocks. It has a good track record in selecting small to medium-sized companies. The annual subscription for the first year is £59.50, rising to £75 thereafter. The publisher's address is Investors Stockmarket Weekly, Garrard House, 2–6 Homesdale Road, Bromley, Kent B22 9WL (Tel: 0181 402 8181).

SYSTEM HOUSE is a monthly review of the financial performance of the UK computing services industry. It is less stock market and more industry-oriented than *Techinvest* and covers most companies in this fast-growing sector of the market. It is specialised and the annual subscription is relatively expensive at £295 per annum. Well worth the money, though, for the managers of sizeable portfolios who are interested in computer-related stocks. (Tel: 01252 724584).

YORKSHIRE FOCUS and *CITY CONFIDENTIAL* specialise in smaller companies and their monthly profiles often trigger a helpful line of thought. The annual subscription is currently £29.50 for the first year and £59.50 thereafter. The publisher's address is Independent Financial Publications, 16 Wells Promenade, Ilkley, West Yorkshire LS29 9LF. (Tel: 01943 600644).

THE FLEET STREET NEWSLETTER is published fortnightly and currently divides its recommendations into three sections. Only the first section covers larger companies. The annual subscription is £45 for the first year and £96 per annum thereafter. (Tel: 01932 354020).

THE PENNY SHARE GUIDE and *PENNY SHARE FOCUS* are both fortnightly newsletters that concentrate upon penny stocks. They can be very rewarding, but penny stocks are often illiquid and the market-makers' spread is very high when expressed as a percentage of the share price. The annual subscription to *The Penny Share Guide* is £25 in the first year, rising to £59.50 in the next. (Tel: 01932 354020). *Penny Share Focus* is £15 in the first year, rising to £59.50 thereafter. The address is Columbus House, 28 Charles Square, London N1 6HT.

All of these newsletters recommend and/or profile specific stocks. There are some other publications which help investors to have a better understanding of the forces that influence the market as a whole. Again, I will list them in order of value for money, assuming that cost is a critical factor:

1. *WALL STREET JOURNAL* is an excellent newspaper. The European version gives a very good five-day-a-week coverage of world markets with particular reference to Wall Street, the most influential of them all.

2. *BARRONS* is a leading weekly American investment publication, which currently costs £3.70 per copy and is well worth every penny.

In particular, the roundtable conferences with investors of the calibre of Peter Lynch, John Neff and Jim Rogers are highly informative, as are the very detailed interviews with leading fund managers. In addition, there are often excellent reflective articles on such subjects as cash flow, price-to-sales ratios and the like.

3. *THE ECONOMIST,* which is published weekly, is an excellent magazine for keeping in touch with world economic and financial developments. I particularly recommend to you the last couple of pages, which highlight Economic and Financial Indicators, showing the performance of world stock markets, money supply statistics, world interest rates, trade balances, reserves, exchange rates, industrial production, GNP, GDP, retail sales, unemployment, consumer and wholesale price movements and wage increases on a week-by-week basis.

4. *THE GLOOM, BOOM AND DOOM REPORT* edited by Dr Marc Faber in Hong Kong (Tel: 00 852 2801 5410) is another fascinating newsletter. He is invariably extremely bearish, which helps to keep one's enthusiasm in check.

5. *THE BANK CREDIT ANALYST* is a monthly newsletter with an excellent record for analysing and determining market trends. Based in Montreal (Tel: 001 514 499 9706) it tends to concentrate on the American market, but, as we all know, that is where trends usually start.

6. *VALUE LINE* is an indispensable tool for investing in American shares. It is the *Company REFS* of Wall Street.

BOOKS ON INVESTMENT

Investment is no different from cooking or gardening. If you wanted to be a better cook or a better gardener, you would not hesitate to read good books, written by the experts who have devoted their lives to those pursuits.

In the UK, there is beginning to be a growing choice of investment books by UK authors, but we still depend, to a large extent, on imports from America. When you consider that some of these books are written by investors of the stature of Peter Lynch, Kenneth Fisher and Martin

Zweig, or are the detailed accounts of the lives and methods of investment giants like Warren Buffett, it is absurd that all aspiring investors do not drink deeply from the fountains of their expertise. In some cases, a lifetime's experience is packed into a couple of books. The time spent reading them should be richly rewarded in superior investment performance in the years ahead.

Primers have already been recommended in Chapter 1. Further reading is listed below and has been classified into three grades: easy to understand post-primer, more advanced and expert only. All the prices mentioned are those prevailing in March 1996 and are for paperbacks, unless otherwise specified.

EASY TO UNDERSTAND POST-PRIMERS

One Up on Wall Street (£11.99) and *Beating the Street* (£9.99), by the very successful fund manager Peter Lynch, give clear guidance on the different types of stocks from slow-growers, turnarounds and cyclicals to fast-growers and asset plays. The American backcloth does not impair the books for UK readers – the approach to investment is universal.

The Midas Touch (£8.99), by John Train, gives an excellent brief outline of the investment principles that have made Warren Buffett America's leading investor.

Both the *Financial Times* and the *Investors Chronicle* agree that my first book *The Zulu Principle* (Hardback, £19.99) 'fills a gap'. There are chapters on selecting growth shares, cash flow, competitive advantage, relative strength, shells, turnarounds, cyclicals and bull and bear markets.

My third book, *PEP Up Your Wealth* (Hardback, £15.99), explains all about PEPs and how to buy high-yielding stocks to beat the market. The system is based on an excellent and very readable American book *Beating the Dow* (£9.99), by Michael O'Higgins and John Downes.

The Crowd/Extraordinary Popular Delusions (£12.95), by Gustave le Bon and Charles Mackay, combines the twin classics of crowd psychology and behaviour in one volume. It should help to remind you that fear and greed are the driving forces of speculation, which have to be controlled by the serious investor.

Reminiscences of a Stockmarket Operator (£11.95), by Edward Lefevre, is an entertaining and instructive biography of a legendary stockmarket operator, Jesse Livermore, showing how important it is not to fight the market, but to go with the force.

The Money Game (£9.99), by Adam Smith, debunks the sacred cows of the investment community in the 1960s. It is not a book about stockpicking, but it is an amusing read, containing many warnings to investors that are still very relevant today.

The Post-War History of the London Stockmarket (£15), by George Blakey, captures the spirit of the times. History can often be the best teacher.

The Investors Guide to Selecting Shares that Perform (Hardback, £25), by a successful UK investor, Richard Koch, has a subtitle 'Ten Ways That Work', which says it all. A helpful guide, outlining the main alternative approaches to investment so that you can choose one that suits your temperament.

How to Make a Killing in the Alternative Investment Market (£12.99), by Michael Walters, the deputy City Editor of the *Daily Mail*, explains the opportunities for private investors in the AIM. The book also includes full details of the smaller and unregulated OFEX market.

FOR MORE ADVANCED READERS

Super Stocks (£14.99), by a leading American investor, Kenneth Fisher, is a superb guide to buying high-technology stocks that have experienced a setback and are due for a massive recovery in their share prices. In particular, Fisher explains in detail the use of price-to-sales and price-to-research and development ratios.

Common Stocks and Uncommon Profits (Hardback, £19.95), by the father of Kenneth Fisher, Phillip Fisher, is a classic work on growth stocks first published in 1958. Even Benjamin Graham recommended it to growth stock investors.

Winning on Wall Street (£10.99), by American investment guru Martin Zweig, outlines his investment philosophy and stock selection and market forecasting measures.

How To Make Money in Stocks (£9.99), by the American investor William O'Neill, contains many good investment ideas and is worth reading, if only for his CANSLIM formula for stock selection.

Accounting for Growth (£14.99), by Terry Smith, is an excellent book on accounting practices that should help you to detect when creative accounting has been at work. In the second edition, the author once again puts company accounts under the microscope.

Keep an eye open, too, for *Corporate Pathology,* another book by Terry Smith due to be published in late 1996. As its name implies, the author analyses the reasons for a number of well-known corporate deaths.

The Craft of Investing (Hardback, £16.99), by John Train, paints with a broad brush and gives some excellent advice on such topics as emerging markets.

The Money Masters and *The New Money Masters* (£10.99 each), by John Train, together with *Market Wizards* and *The New Market Wizards* (£9.99 each), by John Schwager, give very readable accounts of the highly successful strategies of investment giants like Soros, Lynch and Rogers. John Train concentrates more on stock market investors whereas Schwager also covers option, commodity and currency traders. The key point to learn from these books is that almost all of the investors profiled have a method and a discipline that has been honed and tempered by experience.

Profits of the Plunge (£9.99), by Simon Cawkwell, is an amusing account of the experiences of a UK stock market trader and short seller.

Charters on Charting (Hardback, £12.95), by David Charters, explains in simple language why the author believes that charting works and gives precise details of how to do it yourself.

Interpreting Company Reports and Accounts (£21.95), by Geoffrey Holmes and Alan Sugden, is a must for active private investors who want to understand fully the mysteries and complexities of company accounts. The book is constantly being updated, so make sure that you buy the most recent edition.

Buffett – The Making of an American Capitalist (Hardback, £20), by John Lowenstein, is a biography of America's most famous and successful investor. It is very readable and enjoyable and highlights Buffett's fierce ambition and systematic approach. The detailed reasoning behind many of his most successful investments is highly instructive.

Investment Biker (£12.99), by Jim Rogers, is an account of Soros's original partner's trip around the world by motor cycle. In addition to being an interesting and amusing account of his adventures in Russia, China, South America, Africa and the like, it is also interlaced with a great deal of basic investment wisdom.

What Works on Wall Street by Jim O'Shaughnessy is due to be published in September 1996. As the first outsider to gain access to the vast Standard & Poors CompuStat database, he has had a unique opportunity to study the performance of thousands of American shares since 1951.

I know that the author found relative strength in the previous 12 months to be a common factor of all of the most successful systems of share selection. I am keenly looking forward to analysing his other conclusions and comparing them with my own approach.

FOR EXPERTS AND VERY ADVANCED INVESTORS ONLY

The Intelligent Investor (Hardback, £27.99), by Benjamin Graham, is an investment classic which Warren Buffett believes is 'the best book on investment ever written'. The main subjects are 'value investment' and the advantages of a systematic approach. Not a quick and easy read, but full of interesting ideas, which were revolutionary at the time.

Security Analysis (Hardback, £53.95), by Graham and Dodd, is the fifth edition, bringing this investment classic up to date. The book, which is hard going, outlines in great detail the principles and techniques for measuring asset values, cash flow, earnings and other statistics.

Technical Analysis of Stock Trends (Hardback, £57.95), by Robert Edwards and John Magee, is an authoritative book on technical analysis. A very hard read, only for the dedicated.

The Alchemy of Finance (£14.95), by George Soros, is also a hard read and is more for international traders than investors. The main interest is Soros's theory of reflexivity which can be boiled down to 'nothing succeeds like success'.

W. H. Smith, Hatchards or Foyles stock most of these books, but if unsuccessful, try a specialist in books on business and investment, such as Dillons City Business Bookstore, 9 Moorfields, London EC2Y 9AE (Tel: 0171 628 7479) or Books Etc., 30 Broadgate, London EC2 (Tel: 0171 628 8944).

Another easy way of buying investment books is through the Investors Book Club, Analyst, FREEPOST, London EC2B 2GH (Tel: 0171 247 4557). Their catalogue is very comprehensive and all of their books are classified in a helpful way.

INVESTMENT SEMINARS AND MASTERCLASSES

In addition to reading, most private investors would benefit substantially from attending the occasional investment conference or seminar. Sharelink usually organises an excellent one in Birmingham every year and Analyst and Fidelity arrange them occasionally. Hemmington Scott also has an annual get-together in London for REFS subscribers.

In addition to hearing what the various speakers have to say, the extra benefit of attending an investment conference is to meet a large number of other investors who are like-minded and have similar problems and interests. Joining an investment club can also help in this respect, even if you only allocate a small part of your overall funds to it.

For institutions and for active private investors, Rushmere Wynne are now arranging Investment Masterclasses. They will be intensive one-day programmes with lunch, coffee and tea breaks, and wine and canapés afterwards. These breaks are designed to give the delegates an opportunity to meet the speakers and talk with them personally.

In 1996 the price was £495 plus VAT. The speakers will include investors of the calibre of Terry Smith, author of *Accounting for Growth*, Brian Marber, the well-known chartist, and Jeremy Utton, the editor of *Analyst*. Graham Quick of Hemmington Scott will also be speaking about the validation of data and complex issues like the alternative ways of calculating return on capital employed, and I will speak twice and co-ordinate the programme. If you are interested in attending one of these classes, you should telephone Rushmere Wynne on 01525 853726 and ask for a brochure.

20

—

SUMMARY

I hope this book has convinced you that, by being systematic, you will be able to beat the market by a wide margin.

There is nothing magical or mysterious about my method of picking winning growth shares. On the contrary, my approach is rigorous and disciplined. I only buy shares that meet my demanding criteria – some are mandatory, others are highly desirable and the rest can simply be regarded as bonuses.

Here is a summary of my requirements:

A. *MANDATORY REQUIREMENTS*

1.   A PEG of under 1.0 for significant funds and of under about 0.75 for smaller funds.

2.   A prospective PER of not more than 20.

3.   Strong cash flow and, in particular, cash flow per share in excess of EPS for the last reported year and for the average of the previous five years.

4.   Low gearing, preferably under 50%, or, even better, positive cash balances.

5.   High relative strength in the previous twelve months coupled with high relative strength in the preceding month or three months.

6.   A strong competitive advantage.

7.   No active selling by a cluster of directors.

B. *HIGHLY DESIRABLE*

1. Accelerating EPS, preferably linked to the capacity to clone the company's activities.

2. A number of directors buying shares.

3. A market capitalisation in the range of £30m–250m.

4. A dividend yield.

C. *BONUS FACTORS*

1. A low price-to-sales ratio (PSR).

2. Something new.

3. A low price-to-research ratio (PRR).

4. A reasonable asset position.

These criteria can be looked upon as an investor's quiver full of arrows. They do not all need to be fired, some may miss their targets, but you do need to score a substantial number of bull's eyes. The criteria are not meant to be applied rigidly. They are more in the nature of guidelines for growth investors, which taken together help to eliminate dodgy investments and to highlight exceptional investment opportunities. Small infractions of any of the guidelines do not necessarily rule out the shares in question.

Even with mandatory requirements, some flexibility is needed. For example, an attractive prospective investment might not have been awarded a PEG because two years ago its EPS failed to grow by a whisker. However, the company's cash flow might have been double its EPS, its PSR might have been under 1.0 and it might have had a PER of only 12 looking forward to 30% EPS growth during the next few years. In this kind of instance, it would obviously have been absurd to rule out the share because of a minor infraction of the PEG rules two years previously. So it is with all my suggested criteria – massive over-kill on most of the key statistics can more than compensate for a minor worry on just one statistic, particularly if it appears to be an historical blip. Some shares are obviously a raging buy on all counts, but quite frequently the overall attraction of the share has to be weighed up and judgement needs to be exercised in making a final decision.

The essence of my approach for selecting growth shares is to start with the whole universe of the market and sieve it down until only a few remain as candidates for my portfolio. REFS' monthly tables make this task very easy indeed. The fact that a company appears in REFS' tables of lowest PEGs means it has passed through the first sieve – it has at least a short record of EPS growth and there seems to be a good prospect of that continuing.

The second sieve is to set a limit for the PEG. For a very large portfolio, a PEG of under 1.0 is about right, but smaller portfolios can be more selective and a tougher limit can be imposed of, say, 0.75.

The next steps are to check that the prospective PERs of the candidates are not in excess of 20, cash flow is in excess of EPS, gearing is under 50%, and relative strength against the market is positive for the previous twelve months. Relative strength for the previous month should also be positive, but the previous three months is sufficient if the shares appear to be taking a short breather.

Most of these sieves can be ascertained simply by examining the REFS' monthly tables of shares with the lowest PEGs. The exceptions are gearing and three months' relative strength; these can be ascertained from the company entry, which also highlights if directors have been buying or selling their shares.

When some of the mandatory criteria are fulfilled exceptionally strongly, a more tolerant approach can be adopted if some of the other criteria fall a little short. For instance, if cash flow per share were twice EPS, it would not be unduly worrisome if gearing were 70% instead of under 50%. Similarly, if the PEG were 0.5 and a number of directors had been buying a lot of shares, the fact that the PER were 21 instead of under 20 would give me no qualms.

Once the *arithmetical* mandatory criteria are in place, I then seek to identify the competitive advantage that enabled each portfolio candidate to get through all of my sieves. In doing this I use common sense, contact friends who may know something about the business and read press cuttings, brokers' circulars, annual reports and newsflow in the REFS company entry.

At this stage, I also take into account highly desirable supportive factors like accelerating EPS, the company's capacity to clone its activities, whether or not the directors have been buying shares in a big way, the market capitalisation and the dividend yield. I also draw comfort from bonus factors such as a low PSR, something new, a low PRR and a reasonable asset position.

Another invaluable cross-check is the REFS sector analysis to see how the key statistics of the company under review compare with the other companies in its peer group and the sector and market averages.

In the tests made so far, the low PEG method of selecting growth shares has been very successful. In eight tests of six-month periods, shares with PEGs of 0.6 or under were up an average of 22.9%, excluding dividends, against the market's 8.9% calculated on a similar basis. The cash flow sieve had a minimal effect on performance, but provided a degree of comfort. The relative strength sieve improved performance substantially to an average rise of 34.5%.

In thirteen tests with only the one sieve of a PEG of under 0.75, the shares selected from the FT-SE 100 index rose by 21.04% against only 9.53% for the index itself. The Mid-250 stocks with a PEG of under 0.75 also beat their index by a wide margin – an average of 14.8% against 9.56%.

Many investors are surprised by these results. I usually ask them if they can tell me why shares which have a better growth record than the market as a whole, an above-average growth rate in relation to their multiples, better cash flow and better relative strength should not perform better than the market. I have not had a satisfactory answer yet and I am not really expecting one.

I recommend about 10–15 shares as the optimum number for small portfolios, rising to 30 or more for much larger ones. The PEG factor helps to indicate when a share is a buy and also helps to prompt you when the time has come to sell. Many shares can be held for years if they go on doing their thing and the market price does not get overdone. When the PEG rises to over 1.2, you should be on red alert as your safety margin is becoming thinner. Capital gains tax does, of course, have to be taken into account but even with this problem I would certainly be a seller if the PEG reached the market average and I would probably be tempted to sell a little below it. The funds can always be reinvested in another share with a much greater safety margin and with more scope for a major upward status change in its rating.

Do not spend too much time worrying about the market as a whole. Investment is the art of the specific and selection is much more important than timing. If you find that your investments are causing you sleepless nights, sell a few shares down to your sleep level. When you select the shares to be sold, choose the most speculative and those with the highest PEGs. This will improve the average margin of safety of your residual portfolio.

The most important advice I can give private investors is to develop a system, method or discipline of their own. It might be modelled around the kind of ideas I have explained in this book, adapted here and there to meet your personal objectives. Gradually your approach will be refined, honed and tempered by experience. It should never become carved in stone – always be prepared to listen to or read about new investment ideas that may help to improve your knowledge.

Do not listen to stray tips about this or that exciting biotechnology stock or some other concept with little or no record of fundamentals. Very few of them will succeed and most are a recipe for disaster. Run profits, cut losses and use PEPs to the maximum possible extent. Stick to your method and get better and better at operating it. This is the surest road to successful investment.

The point I want to emphasise is that you will get out of investment what you put into it. Read as much as possible about the subject and buy and subscribe to as many weekly and monthly investment products as you can afford. Also, be sure to devote at least an hour or so a week to *thinking* about your investments in a strategic way.

As your technique improves, I predict with confidence that you will begin to enjoy investment as much as any other game that you have learned to play well. The beauty of this particular game, though, is that the more you improve, the richer you will become.

APPENDIX

1. *What Works on Wall Street* by James O'Shaughnessy has now been published. His research based on 40 years of US data from 1954–1994 shows the following results:

	Compound Annual Return %	
	Low value group	High value group
Price-to-Book Value (PBV)	14.4	7.5
Price-to-Cash Flow (PCF)	13.6	6.8
Price-to-Sales Ratio (PSR)	15.4	4.2
Price-Earnings Ratio (PER)	11.2	8.4
EPS up five years in a row and best relative strength	16.86	
PER below 20 and high relative strength	16.66	
High one year relative strength and low PSR	18.14	
High one year relative strength	14.03	
Low one year relative strength	1.78	

To put these figures in perspective the compound annual return for all shares over the 40 year period 1954–94 was 12.5%

O'Shaughnessy did not research the use of PEGs because forecasts were not available over the whole period. However, as you can see, his evidence strongly endorses the other criteria outlined in this book.

2. Jonathan Steinberg, the six times winner of the *Wall Street Journal*'s stockpicking contest, has written *Midas Investing*. His main investment criteria are:

   a) High relative strength and the achievement of new highs.
   b) Insider buying.
   c) Upward revisions and brokers' forecasts.
   d) A strong story.
   e) Strong EPS growth that can be purchased on a low price-earnings ratio. Steinberg regards the PEG as a far more important indicator than the price-earnings ratio and always uses it to decide whether or not a share is a buy. He looks for shares with a growth rate well in excess of the price-earnings ratio. (ie a PEG of well below 1.0.)

   Steinberg's criteria are virtually identical to my own, although I was surprised to see that he did not regard cash flow as critically important. However, in his monthly magazine *Individual Investor*, in January 1997, well after publication of his book, he said that *Individual Investor* had learned from its mistakes and that in future it would be placing increased emphasis on cash flow and balance sheet strength.

3. A piece in Barrons drew attention to research by David Lipshutz of Morgan Stanley. He studied the performance of one thousand of America's largest companies over a period of more than eleven years. He found that companies with the lowest PER in relation to their growth rates (ie low PEGs) **significantly outperformed** the market overall. He also found that the companies with the highest PEGs were the worst performers. 'It is amazing the results were so uniform,' Lipshutz said, 'It shows the power of the concept.'

4. Further support comes from Prudential's Claudia Mott. She calculated PEG ratios for 5041 MidCap stocks going back to 1982. In the 14 years ending in December 1996, she found that MidCap stocks with PEGs of less than 0.75 returned an average of 19.2% a year turning a $1000 investment into an impressive $1166. The average stock with a PEG of between 1.0 and 1.25 grew 16.5% a year during the same period, turning $1000 into $846, while stocks with PEGs of over 2.0 returned just 10.8%, producing a meagre $421. She concluded that shares with a PEG

of under 1.0 were good value, fair value up to 1.25 and over that they became expensive.

5. The four shares I selected using *Company REFS* on 29 November 1995 had appreciated by 29 May 1996 by 64.6% as explained on page 142. Since then, they have continued to gain on the market. By September 1997, the four shares had appreciated by an average of 167% compared with the market's performance of only 29% during the same period.

6. The eight shares in my 1996 New Year's portfolio for the *Financial Mail on Sunday* selected on 29 December 1995, have also continued to beat the market significantly. As you will see on page 148, they had gained 27% by June 1996. By 30 September 1997, the six residual shares (one was sold for a loss of 4% and another was taken over for a profit of 35%) had appreciated by an average of over 100%, against the market's 28%.

7. My son's fund, the Johnson Fry Slater Growth Fund, has continued to increase in value. During 1996, on an offer-to-offer basis, net income reinvested, it was the best performing unit trust in the UK with a gain of 59.1% against the market's 15.7%.

INDEX

Page numbers in italic refer to tables and charts

CREDITS

For supplying and granting permission to quote material, the author and publishers are grateful to the following: Credit Lyonnais Laing, Datastream, Geoffrey Holmes and Alan Sugden, *Interpreting Company Reports and Accounts* (Woodhead-Faulkner), Hemmington Scott for the many extracts from REFS, Conor McCarthy for his insight into the Internet, and Warren Buffett for his many sage aphorisms.